"Impressive book! From the first paragraph, I knew that I would enjoy reading *For Room and Board* about the life of the father of my friend Phil Barkman. The book is a tribute to the transforming love of Jesus Christ that reaches out to all mankind. Mental pictures flooded my mind on every page as I read the life stories that made the man, Atlee Barkman. This was a man who did not use hardship as an excuse for bitterness but rather as a building block to character. So well-written is the account of this man's life that I felt myself grieving at the first mention of his deteriorating health. I wish that I could have known him—someday I will."

— **Martin Mann**

"What a wonderful story of family, faith, determination, and courage! A great picture of how the love of God changes the hearts of men and women."

— **Bill and Jessie Kraft**

"An inspiring story of a man I have always admired. Atlee lived in an era of hard times and experienced difficult life situations. His legacy shows the powerful effect of our choices and points to the overwhelming grace of God! Well-written, and a very good read."

— **Gaylord Barkman**

"Lots of tears and smiles while reading this book. A truly heart-gripping, accurate account of a dear friend of mine. Love you a lot, Atlee Barkman."

— **Alan Raber**

"I did not know Atlee as a young boy, but in later years I got to know him quite well, mostly as a taxi driver, but also as a minister. I remember that when our church was within walking distance from his place, he would walk over to church. After the service, we discussed a lot of Scripture while eating lunch. Atlee had a great concern for the church, but also a good sense of humor."

"Pepper" Andy Miller

"Ok, read the book! I couldn't stop! Cried in chapter fourteen! Laughed out loud in eighteen! A roller coaster ride of emotion in all. The Santa story is my favorite, the perfect attendance award a close second! This book made me proud to have known this man, Atlee Barkman."

Naomi Miller

JPV ❧ PRESS

for Room *and* Board

A Memoir of Atlee Barkman

PHIL BARKMAN

Unless otherwise noted, Scripture is from the Holy Bible, King James Version, Public Domain.

Printed in the United States of America

First Printing, 2018

ISBN 978-1-946389-07-7

JPV ⚡ PRESS

2106 Main Street / PO Box 201
Winesburg, OH 44690

www.jpvpress.com

Dedicated to

the memory of Dad,

and to Mom.

THE COVER

The top photo is of Atlee and his dad, c. 1937.

The lower photo shows Atlee's Bible, his glasses, and the first toy truck that he had. It includes books from Mary's library and a photo of Atlee and Mary in the photo booth at Myer's Lake, c. 1946.

The banner in the middle gives a glimpse of Atlee's sermon notes.

ACKNOWLEDGMENTS

My Heavenly Father, for giving me the opportunity to hear the story of my parents' lives, and the ability to put it to paper.

Sue, for her encouragement, support, and the occasional swift kick.

Elaine, for her accomplished editing that brought this work to its completed state.

Uncle Bert, for his encouragement and the old-timey photos he provided.

Marlin Miller and JPV Press, for bringing this book to publication.

This book has been written to the best of my ability and the extent of my parents' memories. Details have been added, as much in line with their memories as possible.

"See, here I was, then this guy decided that
they could use me this summer, so I went
there. From one to the other.
Whoever needed me."

Attlee Barkman

TABLE OF CONTENTS

"I can't help it!

I get so excited when I start to preach

about the love of God, or any subject.

Just like, heaven, and the heaven of heavens

cannot contain God. I just get excited.

Sometimes I get a little bit loud at home

when I'm by myself. Sometimes I can't sleep

at night, so I think of the Godhead...

ohhh... my tside nuhahmul!

Then I think of the songs;

"Make us pure as thou art," you know.

Then it says we can be made the

righteousness of God in Christ.

All those things make me excited!"

Atlee Barkman

A TRIBUTE

Growing up as Atlee and Mary Barkman's son, I got to see their life first-hand. It was a good life, a simple life; there was hard work, love, laughter, and some hard times. I always appreciated my parents, but as I grew into adulthood, I began to understand more fully the extraordinary lives that Mom and Dad led. I watched them throughout my entire life, and yes, I saw some of the struggles they encountered and the failures they experienced. But I also saw their victories, and their love for God and their family.

The patience, perseverance, and integrity with which they lived their lives have been instructional in my own. They not only taught me well, but also demonstrated to me what it looks like to daily walk with God. The challenges they faced and the grace and love with which they did so made me want to put their story on paper as a tribute to them and as encouragement to others. I hope you enjoy the story of their journey.

— *Phil*

ONE

Propping herself up on her elbow, Lizzie gently eased onto her side. She was almost nine months pregnant, and it wasn't an easy task, but she didn't want to wake John. She hadn't slept well; there just wasn't a comfortable position in which to lie, and the baby had been much more active these last few days. Resting her hand on her stomach, she smiled. Atlee, as they had chosen to name him, seemed to sense her touch and moved again.

She closed her eyes, then sighed; another call of nature. Well, that wasn't unusual. Quietly flipping back the covers, she scrunched into her slippers. It was chilly, and she shivered as she pulled the chamber pot from underneath the bed. This shouldn't take long, but wait... something was not right. Gasping, she clutched at the chair beside her.

"John...!"

But it was already over. Little Atlee had arrived, and the first thing he experienced was not warm, comforting hands welcoming him into the world, but the cold enamel of a worn chamber pot.

Thursday afternoon, 1:00 pm. It's been a late lunch, but a good one; the leftover spaghetti from the restaurant yesterday did not disappoint.

Atlee walks to the living room window and closes the curtain before he sits down. He is eighty-five years old and his eyesight is dimming, but the glare of the sun reflecting off the white garage doors across the street is still bright enough to disturb his nap.

He sinks into his recliner and smiles at his wife, Mary, half curled into her own chair a few feet from his.

"Are you going to nap, too?"

She removes her glasses. "Yes, I think so, I want to be rested in case anybody stops by tonight."

Atlee leans back and closes his eyes. A slight breeze drifts in through the open window, laced with the scent of fresh-mown grass. As he recedes into slumber, a faint image forms in his mind...

The buggy wheels rattle through the gravel, but over the sound, Atlee can hear the clickity-clack of the horse-drawn mower moving steadily through the hay field beside the road. He is five years old, and life has just taken a surprising turn.

Aunt Katie had stopped by the house in Maple Valley where Atlee's family had been living for a year.

Her visit that day was unusual, especially on a workday mid-morning. His mom called Atlee in from the back yard where he had been playing.

"Atlee, I've put your clothes in this bag. You're going to be staying with Aunt Katie and Uncle Dan for a while."

Aunt Katie smiled and motioned. "Come, you're going to be helping us out. I think you'll like it!"

Atlee was puzzled. He liked Aunt Katie and Uncle Dan, but to stay with them? He looked around the kitchen. Not even a good-bye to the others? His father, John, was at work in the Sugarcreek brick-yard and his oldest brother, Albert, was helping a neighbor with his fieldwork. Emanuel and Anna Mae, both older than Atlee, were across the road at the neighbor's house. Only three-year-old Ray-mond was there, playing under the table with a few hand-carved wooden blocks.

Atlee looked back at his mom, but there was no explanation, only a quick hug and a "Now behave yourself!"

Life had not been easy for the Barkman family at their home in Maple Valley, close to the small town of New Bedford, Ohio. Atlee's father was a strong, hard-working man, but it was tough to make a liv-ing in the mid-1930s. It was even more difficult to provide for the family with a portion of his meager income diverted to the purchase of alcohol, a weak-ness he had acquired in his youth. Atlee's mother, Elizabeth (Lizzie), did the best she could with what they had, and Atlee and his siblings helped out as much as possible.

After what seemed to Atlee to be a very long trip, the horse slowly plodded up the steep hill out of the picturesque village of Trail and rounded a corner. Aunt Katie and Uncle Dan's farm came into view. A slight apprehension nudged him. How long would he have to stay here? What would he have to do? Were there any other children around to play with? He kept his questions to himself, however. He had discovered early on that most adults didn't care for too many questions, and they certainly felt no need to explain their actions to a mere child.

As they drove up to the barn, Uncle Dan came out to unhitch the horse. Clutching the small bag containing his few belongings, Atlee followed Aunt Katie across the road and up the short, steep steps to the house.

Entering the side door, Aunt Katie led the way through the kitchen, up the narrow staircase, and down the hall. She twisted the knob on the first door to the right; the hinges creaked as the door opened into a small bedroom. She stepped aside to allow Atlee to enter.

He stopped in the doorway and looked around the room. A small, square window was directly opposite the door, presenting a view of the hillside meadow rising behind the house. Next to the window stood a three-drawer chest with a small woven basket on it. Beside the basket was an oil lamp, the blue trim on its frosted globe worn faint by years of use. Against the back wall was a narrow bed covered with a clean but well-worn patchwork quilt. On the rough wooden floor in front of the bed lay a braided oval rug. A spindle-back chair stood in the corner, with only a hint of its red paint remaining. A few wooden pegs protruded from the wall at shoulder height next to the door. This is where he would hang his pants and shirts.

As Atlee's gaze wandered around the room, the apprehension that he had felt earlier welled up inside of him. The room, even with its furnishings, felt so empty. No big brothers' shoes kicked into the corner, no carved sticks, no unusual stones collected from the creek bed. No clothes thrown carelessly on the bed, which would certainly bring on a scolding from Mom if she saw them. No teasing, no tussling, no scaring each other in the dark after Dad had blown out the lamp at bedtime.

Atlee quickly tossed his bag onto the bed, swallowed the lump in his throat, and descended the stairs to the kitchen, where Aunt Katie had just begun to peel potatoes for supper.

As time passed, he settled into his new home. He had initially expected to be there for only a few days, but weeks passed with no mention of his return home. He finally asked and was told that he would be staying all of summer and fall, possibly into winter.

He was, of course, expected to help out, doing the tasks that a five-year-old boy could do. That wasn't unusual; there had been chores to do at home. So he mowed the yard, fed the chickens, brought in wood for the cook stove, and helped Aunt Katie in the garden.

One of the required tasks was to bring the cows from the pasture to the barn for milking early in the morning. As most children did at the time, Atlee went barefoot all summer and fall, and this meant cold feet, especially on frosty mornings. When he would bring in the cows in the early morning, he would quickly run to a spot where one had just gotten up and warm his feet with the residual body heat from the cow.

It took a bit longer, however, for Atlee to understand why he had been sent away from home. It was not a lack of love or caring on his parents' part, but sheer necessity. There were simply too many mouths to feed. Sending him away relieved some of the pressure, and if by this arrangement Aunt Katie and Uncle Dan received a bit of help, so much the better. While he missed his family, life with Aunt

Katie and Uncle Dan really wasn't too bad. They had no children of their own and treated Atlee as a son.

Being sent away from home to work for room and board meant a lot of changes for Atlee. In the first nineteen years of his life, he made at least seventeen moves from one place to another. He lived with Aunt Katie and Uncle Dan at four different times (at ages five, nine, ten and thirteen) at four locations. During those same years, he also stayed with eight other families for short periods, and at times lived at home with his parents. Moving usually meant going to a new school, and through eight grades, Atlee attended a total of seven different schools.

TWO

There had been several moves in Atlee's life in the five years before he went to live with Uncle Dan and Aunt Katie. He was born on his grandfather Dan Barkman's farm between Charm and Farmerstown. His family then moved to another location closer to Farmerstown, where he briefly attended school at age five. His father, John, lost that home during the Depression, so they moved back to Grandpa Dan's farm for a short time. The next move was to Maple Valley.

Atlee's father, although a member of the Amish church, found it difficult at times to comply with the *Ordnung*, or church rules. Besides his fondness of wine, he would, at times, buy and drive a car.

It was during one of those times that the family headed for Baltic from Maple Valley, with Atlee and Emanuel riding in the rumble seat.

They rounded a corner just as a farmer was driving his cows across the road to pasture. John stepped on the brake pedal, only to discover that the brakes were less than efficient. The car began to slow, but not soon enough, and bumped into a cow. The car wasn't damaged and the cow wasn't injured, but there was a bit of explaining to do. Ownership of cars was forbidden for members of the Amish church.

Their move had brought them to a place where young boys could get their fill of adventure. They explored the woods, roamed the fields, and in the summertime, gigged suckers in the creek with Dad.

They also made a harness out of twine and two of the boys would "hitch" themselves to a little wagon. The others would then sit in the wagon and drive the "horses" around the yard. A little imagination went a long way toward keeping them occupied.

The pace of life in the Barkman household had changed a bit over the last two days. Grandma Barkman had arrived on Wednesday for a visit. It was always fun when she came, but she wasn't there just to entertain the children. It was time to give the house a thorough fall cleaning, and that's when Grandma's expertise and the extra pair of hands were appreciated.

As Mom and Grandma cleared the breakfast table, Dad headed out the door for work and the children scattered in various directions. Early morning sunbeams poked through low-lying clouds, and a fitful breeze swirled muted hues of fall across the yard.

Crossing the narrow dirt road that curved past the house, Atlee and Emanuel wandered through the pasture towards the creek, the dying grass crackling under their bare feet. Accompanied by one of Dad's beagles, the boys followed the creek as it twisted its way toward the trees in the distance. Throwing stones into deep pools, floating stick boats through the "rapids," and once giving chase to a rabbit that was spooked out of a briar patch, the boys used up most of the forenoon with their adventures.

"I wonder if Grandma has a snack for us?" said Emanuel, and the boys trekked towards home.

"Mom! Grandma! We're hungry!" Bursting into the kitchen through the side door, they stopped in their tracks. The curtains had all been removed from the windows, and Mom was standing on a short wooden stool, carefully wiping the glass with crumpled-up newspaper that had been dipped in a solution of water and vinegar. Both boys wrinkled their noses. They had been hoping for a different aroma, maybe that of a pie fresh out of the oven, or at least the rich warmth of coffee soup with brown sugar. But not this time; the tart smell of vinegar mingled with the scent of homemade soap wafting up from the basement where Grandma was washing the curtains.

Mom smiled as she stepped down from the stool.

"I know, boys. I'll get you a piece of bread, and you can each have a little bit of cheese." As she opened the icebox door, they could hear Grandma coming up the basement steps.

Mom and Grandma took a short break from their tasks and sat down with Atlee and Emanuel at the kitchen table. The boys regaled them with tales of their morning wanderings as they enjoyed their snack of bread and cheese, with milk for the boys and coffee for the adults.

Mom wiped the crumbs from the table as the boys headed into the back yard. Running towards the barn, they didn't notice a slightly raised, leaf-covered mound at the edge of the yard. Emanuel dashed through it, with Atlee just a few feet behind.

As Emanuel screamed and fell to the ground, Atlee felt a searing pain engulf his feet. They had run straight through Dad's burn pile. He had burned some trash the evening before, and deep inside the ashes were embers that still glowed red-hot.

Hearing the boys' cries of agony, Mom and Grandma rushed out the door to see both of them lying on the ground, clutching scorched feet. Mom carried them to the porch step as Grandma quickly brought two large bowls of cool water. For the next few hours, the boys sat on the step with their feet in the water and Grandma and Mom hovering over them.

For rural families in the mid-1930s, home remedies were the only practical resource for minor injuries. After cooling off the boys' feet with the water, Grandma went into the basement and re-emerged with a jar of apple butter. She smeared it liberally over the burned areas, then took rags and tied them loosely around the boys' feet, securing the ends around their ankles.

The next few days were a trial for everyone. The boys had to be carried everywhere they needed to go, and the apple butter "dressings" on their feet had to be changed frequently. Fortunately, Grandma stayed for a few days longer than she had planned, taking some of the load off Mom and Dad.

It was mid-afternoon on a Thursday, and Atlee and Raymond had just finished a late lunch. At the time, Atlee was living with his parents and siblings in a house just north of Heini's cheese house in Bunker Hill. At seven years old, Atlee had morning and evening chores to do, but afternoons were often open for play.

As the boys wandered up the road toward the store on top of the hill, they saw Ward, one of the neighborhood "big boys." Ward was already a teenager, but he often hung out with the Barkman boys since there weren't too many other children of his age in the area.

The sunlight glinted off a long, slender object that Ward was holding, and the boys' eyes widened.

His BB gun! Ward had brought it around before and let the boys play with it, but that was a rare treat. Dad had a few guns and did some hunting, but a BB gun for the boys was a luxury they could not afford.

As they approached, Ward took aim at a sparrow pecking at a splash of spilled grain by the road. *Pop!* The little bird flew away unharmed.

Atlee laughed and Ward scowled.

"Think you can do any better?" he challenged, handing the BB gun to Atlee.

The steel tube barrel was dented and scratches crisscrossed the dark wooden stock, but to Atlee and Raymond, the gun was a thing of beauty. Atlee enthusiastically worked the lever action that pumped more air into the chamber and then took careful aim at a glass bottle in the ditch. A squeeze of the trigger, and it was Ward's turn to laugh.

"Not as easy as you thought, huh?"

The boys spent the next few hours on the back roads and in the fields surrounding Bunker Hill, plinking at various targets. The sun sank toward the hilltops and it was time to hand the gun back to Ward, but oh, how the boys wanted that BB gun!

"Can... can we keep it for tonight?" asked Atlee.

Ward shrugged, opened his mouth to comment, and then paused. He looked at them thoughtfully for a moment, then grinned.

"You can keep it for good if you really want it, but you'll have to let me shoot you both in the butt!"

Now it was Atlee and Raymond's turn to pause. A BB to the rear sounded a trifle unpleasant, but was possession of this treasure worth a small and hopefully fleeting discomfort?

"Not from this close, though, right?" asked Atlee.

"Nah, go over in the yard, and I'll let ya have it from here," responded Ward with a chuckle.

Raymond's eyes were wide as they crossed the ditch and headed into the yard.

"You know you can't cry!" Atlee hissed under his breath.

"Okay, right there," called Ward, and the boys stopped and held their breath.

Pop! from the road, and Atlee twitched as he felt the sting of a fast-moving BB. Rubbing the spot, he turned towards Raymond.

"That wasn't bad at all!" he said, secretly hoping that Ward would miss his next shot. Another *Pop!* and a loud "*Oww!*" from Raymond told him he had hoped in vain.

Ward was laughing, quite pleased with his shenanigans, as he handed the BB gun to the boys. Atlee's hand closed around the cool metal of the gun barrel, and he realized the momentary pain was quite worth the gain.

He and Raymond were now the proud owners of their very own BB gun!

THREE

One day Atlee and his brother Emanuel were playing by the water trough. Standing close by was the cart that was used to haul the milk cans out to the road. The cans were then placed on a platform to make it easier for the milkman to load them into his truck.

As Emanuel stood on the front end of the cart, it tipped, throwing him off. He struck his chin on the water trough and almost bit off the entire front of his tongue.

Atlee's father John

Dad was at work at Heini's Cheese when this happened. He was in the process of removing a massive wheel of cheese from a rack when he was told the news about Emanuel's injury. Rattled, he dropped the cheese, and it shattered on the floor. His boss told him not to worry, to just go and take care of his son. The boss cleaned up the ruined cheese.

Before leaving for work one morning, their dad told Atlee and Raymond to go to the neighbor, "Apple Butter" John, to bring home some straw. They used a rope sling to carry the straw. The sling was a web of rope that was laid on the ground and piled high with straw. Then the ends were gathered, holding the straw securely and creating a bundle that could be carried on the back.

The boys, however, drank some of Dad's hard

cider before going to John's farm. They got there, loaded up the straw, and managed to lose most of it before they got home. Atlee was only seven years old at the time.

Atlee and his brothers noticed a white pigeon in their barn, along with the other grey pigeons. After luring her with grain, they finally had Polly, as they named the bird, eating from their hands. Polly became a pet

Atlee pulling, Raymond pushing

and would sit on their hands, allowing them to carry her around. When winter came and the boys went sled riding, Polly would sit on the front of the sled and ride along. She was, as far as Atlee knew, the only sled-riding pigeon in the history of Holmes County.

At eight years old, Atlee developed a fever that home remedies did not seem to cure. His parents became more concerned as a headache and rashes followed the fever. He began to complain of nausea, and had trouble swallowing.

Realizing that this was more than just a common cold or the flu, his mom and dad took him to the doctor in Millersburg. In spite of being sick, Atlee was fascinated by the town. In 1938, Millersburg felt like a big city to a little Amish boy from the country.

After a thorough examination by the doctor, Atlee was diagnosed as having rheumatic fever. This was a frightening diagnosis, as rheumatic fever had the potential of causing life-long consequences, among them being damage to the heart valves.

The doctor sent Atlee home with his parents after prescribing the appropriate medications. It was almost a month before Atlee fully recovered, with no long-term effects.

The years of living at various homes produced many experiences for Atlee, both good and bad. One of the more shocking incidents occurred when he was living with his Aunt Fannie's family. He was eight years old and attending Boyd's School on

County Road 201. It was a clear, bright fall morning as Atlee and his friends Helen and Eli walked to school. The cool breeze blowing briskly across the fields pushed back the thought of the tedious hours ahead in the classroom.

Seeing the empty pasture field to their left, Helen said, "Hey, no cows in the field today. Let's cut across."

"Yeah, we'll have time to play catch before school starts," replied Atlee.

The fence was a single strand of electric wire, and the farmer had told them it would be turned off when the cows were not in the field.

Atlee grasped the wire, intending to lift it up for the others to slip through underneath. The moment his hand closed over it, however, a burning shock jolted up his arm. Not only was the electricity turned on, it was not pulsing, and a steady stream was flowing through the fence.

He tried frantically to open his hand, only to find that his muscles were convulsing and his hand was locked onto the wire.

"C'mon, hold it up a little higher," said Helen, as she ducked to slide underneath. One look at Atlee's face, though, and she could see something was very wrong.

"Is it on? Let go!"

Atlee couldn't move, he couldn't speak, and his thoughts blurred.

"We gotta do something!" exclaimed Helen. "Can we cut the wire?" Eli grabbed Atlee's arm and tried to pull him away from the fence, but only succeeded in pulling the fence post out of the ground.

Eli knew that it was only a matter of time before Atlee would suffer serious injury. Fortunately, he was wearing a pair of rubber-soled boots, so he stepped on the section of wire that was between Atlee and the barn, pushing it to the ground. This caused the current to run into the ground, freeing his friend.

As the burning sensation in his arm ceased, Atlee slowly, painfully, opened his hand just enough to pull it off the wire. Then, disoriented, he grabbed onto it again with his other hand. Eli still had the wire pushed to the ground, giving Helen the chance to pull Atlee's hand off the wire and guide him away from the fence.

He stood motionless for a moment, then sank to his knees, his body drained of strength. Every breath was an effort as he struggled to recover from the shock. Helen and Eli gathered around him.

"Are you okay? Man, that was close. Nearly

knocked you out, huh?"

It was a few minutes before Atlee could speak or get to his feet. Finally, with muscles relaxing and color returning to his cheeks, he stood up.

"Well, I guess there isn't much time left for catch, is there?" he said, and the others laughed, relieved that he was all right. They headed down the road towards school.

"I wonder why old man Weaver didn't turn off that fence," Eli said. "Maybe we'll have to knock over a few of his corn shocks some night."

Atlee didn't reply. His hand still ached, and the memory of that helpless feeling was too fresh in his mind. They arrived at school, and for once, he was glad to just slide into his seat and relax. There was going to be plenty of time to play catch some other day.

It was Thursday morning on the Aden Miller* farm. The chores were done, and breakfast was almost over. Aden drained his coffee cup, wiped his mouth with the back of his hand, and said, "Atlee, don't forget to churn that butter before you head to school."

Atlee nodded. There were always chores to do,

no matter where he was staying, and it was no different here. On the day that Aden's wife butchered chickens, he had to help catch them before school. He arrived at school late and with a number of scratches on his arms. The other children found great humor in this, and for a while, they called him "Hingle Ducta" (Chicken Doctor).

Churning was one of his morning tasks on the Miller farm, and he hadn't forgotten it yet. He tugged his jacket a bit tighter as he stepped outside. The stiffening breeze brought with it the chill of coming winter, and he hurried across the yard to the milk-house. As he entered, he stooped to pet the five little puppies huddled in the corner on a couple of old gunnysacks. They tumbled happily over each other at his approach. It was his job to feed them, and they eagerly expected another meal.

"Not now, guys, you already had breakfast!" Giving their soft fur a final ruffle, he turned to the butter churn. It was an old barrel churn with a crank, and making butter was one of his easier chores. He tapped lightly on the plug. After many years of use, it had become worn and was now wrapped in a rag to make sure it sealed.

Atlee twisted the crank for a few minutes and then paused as a dilemma presented itself. Should he answer the call of nature, or just quickly finish churning? After a few more turns of the handle, nature won out. It took just a quick trip to the barn, and Atlee returned to the milk-house to finish his job.

One step through the door, though, and he stopped in his tracks. The puppies didn't come running to meet him. They were lined up side-by-side, enthusiastically lapping up the puddle of cream that spread across the floor.

Atlee's heart sank. Butter was an important staple of farm life, and neither Mr. nor Mrs. Aden was going to be happy about this. But how could it possibly have spilled? He had checked the plug and it had been tight, with the rag around it... and then he realized what had happened. The rag had dangled close to the floor, and the mischievous puppies had managed to pull it out.

Well, there was no help for it; Aden had to be told. Atlee found him in the barn, hitching up the horse for a trip to town, and began to explain.

"I think the puppies pulled on the rag..." As he continued, Aden's face darkened with displeasure.

"So you're going to blame the dogs, huh? You think I'm going to buy that? You're just too darn lazy, and you think you can get away with not churning today!"

With that, his hand fell roughly on Atlee's shoulder and pushed him against the side of the stall. His other hand found the rein that he was about to hook to the bridle, and he swung it against Atlee's legs. The sting of the leather burned through his thin pants, and Atlee bit his lip to keep from crying out. His dad had administered a number of spankings already, but usually that was with a switch, not a leather strap. The blows continued until Aden felt that justice had been done.

"Now go clean up that mess!"

Atlee returned to the milk-house, tears streaming down his face. It just wasn't fair, but there was nothing he could do but take the punishment and obey. The puppies weren't playful anymore. Stuffed to the brim with rich cream, they were sprawled over each other in the corner, oblivious to the injustice they had caused. Atlee cleaned up what was left of the cream, washed the churn, and then, after washing his face, headed to school.

*Names have been changed

FOUR

While living with Uncle Dan and Aunt Katie on a farm north of Fryburg, Atlee attended the school in Fryburg. This schoolhouse is now the church building on the corner of State Route 241 and County Road 201.

The time that Atlee spent tending livestock on various farms generated a concern and care for animals. One scene that never left his memory was the day a cow over-indulged on alfalfa and became bloated. Uncle Dan took a knife and inserted it into the cow's stomach between the third and fourth ribs, relieving the pressure.

Atlee always called cows his rain gauge. If they were lying down in the field, it would rain within twenty-four hours.

"There's my rain gauge, right there, lying there... those cows. It's likely to rain in twenty-four hours. It might not be much... See, you don't need a newspaper or a radio to know what the weather's going to be."

He was especially drawn to horses and developed great skill in handling them. At nine years old, he was deemed old enough to drive on his own. One day he was driving one of Uncle Dan's horses hitched to a "hack." As he approached home, the horse took off running, and Atlee couldn't hold her. Turning into the driveway, they faced the gate, a single wooden pole. The horse cleared the pole with her front legs and then stopped abruptly. Atlee managed to keep his seat despite the sudden stop, and no harm came to horse or gate.

One of the most vivid memories from Atlee's time on that farm was of an event in the summer of 1939. Uncle Dan's farm was located in a narrow valley that ran north and south. The house was on the gentle slope of the hillside to the east, while the barn was on the valley floor, located between two creeks. The larger stream rushed along on the west side of the valley, and the smaller one meandered down from the east. A narrow gravel road curved by the south side of the farm, with a rickety bridge over each creek.

It was a warm summer evening, and Atlee and Uncle Dan noticed the wind increasing as they finished the chores.

"Looks like there's a storm coming," said Uncle Dan as they walked to the house. The wind tugged at their clothes as it whipped around them. A bank of storm clouds churned in from the west, just above the trees that crowned the ridge, and twilight arrived early. Uncle Dan and Atlee quickened their steps as the first drops of rain pelted them. Hurrying into the house, they quickly closed the windows.

They sat down to the supper Aunt Katie had prepared and had scarcely begun to eat when the storm struck. Rain lashed at the windows, lightning marched across the fields, and booming thunder rattled the windows.

Half an hour passed as they enjoyed their supper. The wind died down and the thunder and lightning moved on, but the rain continued to fall.

Darkness had arrived with the storm, and although they could not see the rising creek, the rush of water could be heard above the sound of the falling rain.

Atlee helped Aunt Katie clear the table and wash the dishes, and then they joined Uncle Dan in the living room. Aunt Katie patched a pair of pants while Uncle Dan read the newspaper. Atlee pulled a book from Aunt Katie's collection and sat on the couch to read. Uncle Dan peered out the window into the blackness and then tried to focus on his paper again. Finally, he folded the paper and thoughtfully rubbed his chin.

"Well, Katie, I'm thinking we should probably not stay here tonight. Hard telling how high the water's going to get."

Aunt Katie glanced at Atlee. She had grown increasingly concerned about the possibility of flooding, but had not wanted to show it.

"So what should we do? Go up to Big Mose's place?" Big Mose and his wife lived a bit farther up the valley and their house, located almost on top of the ridge, was safe from flooding.

"I think we had better," replied Uncle Dan. "We're going to get wet, but that beats getting washed away."

Atlee didn't say anything as he went to get his jacket and hat. He felt a thrill of excitement at the thought of an adventure with the faint possibility of danger thrown in.

Aunt Katie blew out the lamps as Uncle Dan lit the lantern, and they headed out the back door and across the yard. The rain was heavy, and the dim light of the lantern shone little more than a few feet ahead. Uncle Dan led the way through the gate and then across the narrow footbridge that spanned the smaller creek. It wasn't a trickle anymore; the black water rushed by just inches below the bridge.

They followed the path that ran alongside the pasture fence, then turned and headed uphill, through the wet, clinging grass of the field that sloped up to Big Mose's house.

It was a miserable walk. They were soaked to the skin in minutes, and the rain and darkness obscured all landmarks. The grass on the steep hillside was slick, and maintaining their footing was a struggle. Atlee gripped Aunt Katie's hand as she followed the feeble flicker of the lantern.

Suddenly, the light of the lantern showed Big Mose's barn. With just a few steps more, they would have walked right into it. By-passing the barn, they squished across the yard toward the friendly glow of a lamp gleaming through the farmhouse window.

Uncle Dan knocked, and in a minute Big Mose opened the door with a surprised look on his face.

"Dan! Katie! Come in out of the rain, folks; you're soaked! What happened? Did you get flooded out?"

Uncle Dan wiped the water out of his eyes and shook his head.

"Not yet, but I'm thinking it might happen by morning if this rain keeps up."

"Well, you folks come on in, get dried off, and we'll find some room for you to sleep."

Big Mose's wife put a pot of coffee on to boil as Uncle Dan, Aunt Katie, and Atlee dried off. Then they all gathered in the living room, and the grown-ups started discussing the severity of the storm.

Atlee's mind wandered. How were things back on the farm? Were the chickens and the cows going to be okay? And what about the horses? He sure didn't want anything to happen to them. And what if the house would wash away? Where would they go then? He wondered about Mom and Dad. Were they okay? How was all this going to end? The concerns weighed heavily on his mind as he drifted off to sleep on a blanket in the corner of the living room.

"Atlee, wake up! Come here, I want to show you something." Uncle Dan was bent over him, nudging his shoulder.

Atlee squinted in the morning light and pushed back the blanket. Getting to his feet, he followed Uncle Dan out the front door and around to the south side of the house, overlooking the valley. The rain had passed, and a breeze, heavy with the scent of wet earth, was blowing gently up the hillside.

"Look at that!" Uncle Dan swept his arm to the south, and Atlee's eyes widened. Where once there had been two creeks, there was now a river covering the valley floor. Their house was just out of reach of the brown, swirling water, but the barn stood like a man-made island in the torrent. The road crossing the valley was underwater, and both bridges had been swept away. All of the fences in the torrent's path were gone, knocked down by the rush of water and debris.

Atlee, Uncle Dan, and Big Mose walked down to the farm and cautiously waded through the swift-flowing water and into the barn.

Atlee stood inside, the water nearly to his waist, looking at the debris floating around him. Buckets, a milking stool, and soggy straw swirled through the barn. He sloshed through to the horse stalls, wanting to make sure they were all right. Much to his relief, they were fine, although a bit spooked. As he turned to leave the horses, he was astonished to see the heavy, wooden feed bin slowly floating through the center of the barn.

Clear, beautiful days came after the storm. Cleanup was done within a week, and the fences had been repaired. Life returned to normal. Many times, though, as Atlee scooped up grain for the horses, he would marvel at the amount of water it had taken to float that massive wooden feed bin. That night had been a bit scary, but at least no harm had come to them or any of the animals.

FIVE

Atlee lived in at least three different places during the year he was nine. One of these locations was the Feikert farm on Township Road 605, a mile or so north of Beechvale. Often, these changes also brought a change of school.

While living with his parents in Bunker Hill, Atlee attended North Bunker Hill School, on the northeast corner of the intersection of County Road 77 and Township Road 207. The old schoolhouse where these stories occurred is now a studio at Heini's Cheese in Bunker Hill.

It was the last day of school. The excitement was high as the bell rang, calling the children in from the schoolyard. As they settled into their seats, it was evident that today was less about learning and more about wrapping up the school year. The scores of the year-end tests would be announced today, along with grade passes and fails.

The *tap tap* of teacher Loil Brown's ruler on his desk quieted the room. Following the Pledge of Allegiance and a few songs, Mr. Brown passed out the awards for best grades. Then came a surprise.

"I have another prize to give. Atlee, come up front, please."

Atlee hesitated. He hadn't expected an award for his grades and couldn't think of anything else he had done that was worthy of a prize. He slid out of his seat and shuffled to the front of the room. As he shifted from one foot to another, Mr. Brown held out a small paper bag.

"Congratulations, Atlee! You are the only student this year to not miss a single day of class. Here are a few gifts for you."

Atlee's face grew warm as his classmates cheered. He hadn't given any thought to the fact that he had gone to school every day.

He turned toward his desk, but stopped as his

friends shouted, "Open it! Open the bag!"

Mr. Brown nodded. Atlee carefully unfolded the tight crease along the top. The slight crinkle was music to his ears. Cautiously he peered into the bag, and his eyes widened. A bright yellow pencil and a large pink eraser lay across the bottom. Alongside was a pack of Wrigley's Doublemint chewing gum. Underneath the gum was a Wally Berger baseball card. Atlee grabbed the gum and waved it in the air, grinning, and then fished out the pencil, the eraser, and the card.

Mr. Brown smiled.

"What else do you have in the bag?"

Atlee placed his gifts on Mr. Brown's desk and reached into the bag again. In his excitement, he had overlooked a small, round, cardboard container with a lid. Puzzled, he pulled it out. Turning it, he read the words on the side: JACKS. Jacks! Ten jacks and a bright red ball! Pulling off the lid, he was about to dump them on the desk when Mr. Brown held up his hand.

"Not now, Atlee. I think you will have time for that at recess."

"Okay. And thank you, Mr. Brown!"

Atlee gleefully plunked the gifts into the bag and returned to his seat. He placed the pencil in the groove on top of his desk, with the eraser beside it. Carefully wrapping the jacks and the gum inside the bag, he placed it in his desk. He sat still for a moment and then raised his hand.

"Yes, Atlee?"

"Thanks for my gifts, Mr. Brown!"

The teacher's eyebrows arched briefly.

"Why sure, Atlee; you deserve them."

Atlee could hardly wait until recess. At Mr. Brown's dismissal, he grabbed his jacks and sat down by the steps with a few of his friends, and a fast-paced game was soon underway. It seemed like only a few minutes until the bell rang. Scooping the jacks back into the container, he hurried into the classroom and up to Mr. Brown's desk.

"Mr. Brown, those gifts are really spiffy! I sure didn't expect to get anything just for being in school every day."

Mr. Brown rested his elbows on the desk, his fingertips forming a peak in front of his goateed chin. He regarded Atlee thoughtfully for a moment, then leaned back in his chair.

"Well, Atlee, those gifts seem to be a bit over-whelming for you, don't they? If you wish, I could take back one or two."

Atlee took a step back. That was not what he

had expected at all! Opening his mouth to protest, he caught the twinkle in the kindly eyes and grinned.

"Aw shucks, Mr. Brown, I just... I was just... well, thanks!" He turned and hurried back to his seat, placing the jacks safely inside the desk again. The pencil and eraser were put to good use, one piece of gum was shared with Raymond (the rest he carefully rationed over the next few days), and the jacks provided entertainment for the entire summer. It was the first time Atlee had received gifts in school, and that day became a treasured memory.

Atlee attended the same school a few years later. Then, Simon Sommers was the teacher. Mr. Sommers gave him a hard time about something, so for two afternoons in a row, Atlee snuck out of the schoolhouse into an adjoining field and hid behind the corn shocks till the others came by after school. He was afraid that Mr. Sommers would make him stay after school. Apparently there was no punishment for the sneaking out.

Mr. Sommers also tried to make Raymond write with his right hand instead of his left, so their mom told Atlee to tell the teacher to leave Raymond alone. Problem solved.

Atlee lived with Dan and Katie for a time on a farm west of Holmesville. They moved there on a Saturday in August and spent Sunday relaxing and resting.

Weeks passed, and life settled into a routine. One evening as Aunt Katie cleared the supper dishes from the table, she glanced at Atlee and smiled.

"Well, Atlee, are you ready for school tomorrow?"

A chill ran through him. He had been too busy to think about going to school. Now there would be another school, another teacher he didn't know, and other children that were not his friends and would probably never be. He didn't say a word as he trudged up the stairs to his bedroom. The bed frame creaked as he collapsed onto the lumpy mattress and stared into the darkness.

His mind wandered, and he thought of the friends he had made in the Maple Valley, Farmerstown, and Boyd schools. They would be going to their classes together, learning, laughing, and playing, and it would all happen without him. Well, this time would be different. He was not going to school! There was plenty of work on the farm, and Uncle Dan would be glad to have him around all day to help out.

Atlee slept fitfully that night, fragments of

dreams flickering through his sleep. He felt groggy and tired when Uncle Dan woke him in the morning. His stomach was tight with anxiety as he picked at his breakfast. Would they really allow him to stay at home? Uncle Dan headed out to the barn, and Atlee's question was soon answered as Aunt Katie said, "Atlee, go comb your hair. The bus will be here soon."

He shook his head. "I'm not going."

She glanced at him. "Don't be silly! Of course you're going. You can't just stay at home, you know."

"But I can! I can help Uncle Dan with the all the work that needs doing."

She sighed and tucked a stray strand of hair back under her covering. "Just stop it, okay? You can't stay home, and that's final! And look, there's the bus now. C'mon, I'll walk you out."

She took his hand and walked with him through the front door as the big yellow bus pulled to a stop in a swirl of dust. He looked up at the faces of strangers peering out the windows. A suffocating fear welled up inside of him. Jerking his hand out of Aunt Katie's grasp, he burst into tears.

"I am NOT going to go!"

Aunt Katie reached for his arm, but he pulled away and slumped onto the grass. She gripped his elbow and tried to pull him to his feet, but he twisted away.

"Atlee, get up right now! Stop this nonsense and listen to me..."

Atlee rolled away from her and lay face down on the grass, sobbing. After a few minutes of Aunt Katie's unsuccessful entreaties, the driver stepped down from the bus.

"Do you need a hand, ma'am?"

"I don't know what to do," said Aunt Katie. "He won't listen."

"Well, let's each take an arm, and we'll get him on the bus."

Grasping an arm apiece, they lifted Atlee up from the ground. Not about to give in so easily, he struggled, kicked, and cried as they half dragged, half carried him to the bus. The driver pushed him up the steps.

"Go find a seat and sit down, son."

Atlee stumbled to the first empty seat he saw and sat down, his face in his hands. Fear and embarrassment coursed through him as the bus rattled down gravel roads, picking up more children. To his relief, nobody sat with him.

When they arrived at the school, he trailed the other children into the classroom. He looked around and saw that he was the only Amish child in the room, and at recess, he discovered that he was also the only Amish in the entire school. At that time, there were almost no Amish living anywhere west of Holmesville.

He knew no one and had no friends. Seeing that nobody played on the slide, he climbed up and slid down. It was something to do, so he kept on doing that at every recess. Climb the ladder, scoot down, climb the ladder, scoot down.

He watched the others play softball and prisoner's base but didn't dare join them. Then, back to the slide. Finally, after three awkward and lonely days, he acquainted himself with some of the other students and eventually ended up making friends, as he would do in many other situations throughout his life.

Atlee's Uncle Abe stayed at this farm with Dan and Katy for a period of time. He was slightly handicapped, and one time he chased after Uncle Dan with a pitchfork. No harm was done, though.

Abe also stayed with Atlee's parents at one point. He had a stubborn streak, but he would listen when John told him to do something. One evening, John took Abe up to his bedroom for the night. Abe hadn't wanted to go, but John took him inside the room and then left, closing the door.

The next morning when John went to wake Abe, he found him right inside the door. Abe was standing exactly where John had left him the night before, his feet swollen from his all-night stand.

Abe did have a unique talent. While unable to play a musical instrument, he could play tunes on the armrest of his chair, using only his fingers and the heels of his hands.

SIX

Mid-summer, 1941. Atlee, now eleven years old, contemplated the large garden plot beside the driveway. The sun beat down from a cloudless sky, the heat of its rays barely relieved by the fitful breeze that whispered through the growing corn.

Atlee was staying with his Aunt Barb and her family. Aunt Barb had a medical condition that required surgery, so she and Uncle Jake were taking the whole family with them to Columbus.

They left Atlee at home alone with instructions to weed the "patch."

As the car carrying the family pulled away, Atlee trudged out the driveway to the garden. It looked huge; it would take all day to get it done. Not only was it a large garden, but it also had been neglected for some time, and the weeds were at least two feet tall. He would've liked to go along to Columbus, but that was not an option. His job was to pull the weeds. He looked around. Home was miles away, and loneliness tugged at his heart.

A tear trickled down his cheek as he knelt and began weeding. As he moved down the row, a wave of homesickness rolled over him, and the tears came faster. He looked around again. There wasn't anybody close by to see him cry, but he felt so exposed. Running to the barn, he sat on a bale of straw and buried his face in his hands, sobbing. Life just didn't seem fair. Why did he have to be here when he missed his family so much?

A few minutes passed and the tears slowed. Well, there was a job to finish, and that was that. He went out to the garden and began pulling weeds again, but the breeze only seemed to bring more memories of home. Over the next few hours, his task was interrupted numerous times by trips to the barn to vent his tears of loneliness.

That afternoon stayed fresh in Atlee's memory for years to come.

Atlee's skill in farming increased even through his pre-teen years. At that time, most farmers used horses, which was fine with him. There were few things that he enjoyed more than working with a good team or driving a fast horse.

At eleven years old, Atlee helped out on the farm of his mother's brother, Will Miller. Atlee's most unpleasant chore at the Millers' was to wash out the baby's soiled diapers, scrubbing them until they were clean. But there were some fun times, too. Uncle Will often took a nap after lunch. Taking advantage of his snooze, Atlee and his two cousins, Jonas and Abe, would hurry outside and hitch up two goats in a homemade harness made of baler twine. They would then hook them to a little wagon and drive them around the barnyard. At fourteen years of age, Atlee would return to this farm to help out.

In the fall of 1942, Atlee began working at the Henry Mast farm west of Mount Hope, close to the intersection of two township roads, 229 and 607.

He was twelve years old and made $12 per month. The money, of course, went to his parents.

One of Atlee's memories of the Henry Mast farm was the labor that was involved in the spreading of lime on the fields. A load of lime would be brought to the farm and dumped beside the barn. When it was time to fertilize the fields, the lime would be shoveled onto a wagon that had a spreader attached to the back.

It was a two-man job to get the lime onto the fields. One person drove the horses, and another stood in the lime at the back of the wagon and shoveled it into the spreader. It was dusty work, and even a slight breeze would swirl clouds of lime dust through the air, coating both driver and shoveler.

One day while Atlee was driving the team and Henry was shoveling the lime into the spreader, the pin securing the wagon tongue slipped out. The horses spooked and, before Atlee could get a better grip on the reins, took off running. With the singletrees banging around their hind legs, the team headed through the fields toward home. Atlee and Henry knew that some of the children might be playing outside, and they were concerned for their safety. Hurrying after the runaways, they were relieved to see that the horses had run back to the barn and stopped. No one had been in danger.

One evening there was a big ice cream supper planned at the Brown School north of the Mast farm. Atlee was desperate to go, but nobody in the Mast family was interested. Henry gave Atlee permission to go, if he could find a way to get there. The Mose Nisley family lived close by and was going to the supper, so Atlee asked if he could ride along. Mose said he could, but he'd have to stand on the back of the buggy. Atlee happily agreed and rode all the way to the school, clinging tightly to the buggy frame. It felt a bit uncomfortable to be at the supper, as he didn't know anybody except the Nisley family. He did, however, get to eat his fill of ice cream, so it really didn't matter.

It was during this time that a series of events changed Atlee's life forever. He made the acquaintance of two brothers, Ammon and Joe Swartzentruber, and they became close friends. The boys spent much of their spare time together, along with Atlee's younger brother Raymond. Atlee also began to spend time with Ammon and Joe's family. Andy and Amanda—Ammon and Joe's parents—made him feel right at home. There were three more Swartzentruber children: Eli, the eldest son, and two girls, Nettie and Mary.

The Swartzentruber boys were talented musicians, and much time was spent singing and playing guitar and harmonica. One evening as Atlee was approaching their house, he heard what he assumed was a radio. As he turned into the driveway, he looked up to see the siblings on the front porch, playing their instruments and singing.

One of Mary's earliest memories of Atlee was on a Sunday after church. He was standing at Joe's buggy with his foot propped up on the hub of the wheel, talking to Joe. Mary was also in the buggy, but there wasn't much of a connection then. Mary said that Atlee, being rather short, could hardly get his foot high enough to reach the hub, but he got it done.

On an early spring Sunday in 1943, Atlee had just finished lunch with his family in Bunker Hill. A fresh breeze nudged puffs of cloud across a vast expanse of blue. There was nothing for Atlee to do till the evening chores, so he headed up the hill towards the general store on the corner. That's where his buddies would be if they were free.

Sure enough, John, Zack, and Bill were at the store, discussing what the day's adventure could be. Atlee joined them, and they began a leisurely stroll towards Berlin. There was no excitement to be found in town, so they headed east along State Route 39.

As the afternoon stretched on, the boys encountered the buggies of those going home from church. The occasional car rattled by, raising clouds of dust. They were approaching the intersection of State Route 39 and County Road 77 when Zack looked up at the high bank on the right.

"Hey, let's get up on top of there and chuck a few rocks at buggies!"

The boys looked at each other. Was he serious? The hesitation didn't last long, however, and they quickly stuffed their pockets with gravel stones and scrambled up the bank. Stationing themselves along the top, they huddled in the tall grass and waited. It wasn't long before the crunch of gravel announced the approach of their first target. It was a young couple, the reins slack in the husband's hand and his foot dangling out of the buggy as the horse ambled along.

"Now!" whispered Bill, and the boys let fly with their hand-propelled ammunition. One stone missed, two hit the top of the buggy, and another struck the horse on the front shoulder. The horse twitched, then broke into a run as the young man's "Hey!" carried up to the boys on the bank. Oblivious to the danger a runaway horse can cause, the boys laughed as the buggy careened down the road.

A few more buggies passed by carrying two teenage girls, a family with three children, and an elderly couple. All received a barrage of stones, with similar results: startled horses, exclamations of surprise from inside the buggies, and a dramatic increase in speed.

With the last of the stones in their hands, the boys watched as another buggy approached carrying a middle-aged couple. The horse was at a fast trot, and Atlee said, "Okay, we gotta make this count!" As the horse dashed by below, the boys stood up and hurled all the stones they had left.

Every one of them scored a hit, but the boys' glee vanished as they heard a loud "Whoa!" from the buggy. Gravel scattered as the horse slid to a halt. Ducking into the grass, the boys peered over the edge just in time to see the driver exit the buggy in a single leap, agitated face upturned to spot their location.

"Let's go!" hissed Bill, and the boys sprinted for the woods behind them. Dodging low-hanging branches, Atlee glanced over his shoulder just in time to see their pursuer heave himself over the top of the bank. Atlee and his friends had too much of a head start, though, and the man turned and headed back to his buggy.

After giving him sufficient time to leave the area, the boys spent another few hours meandering towards home, the excitement over for the day.

When asked—at age eighty-six—why he did it, Atlee chuckled and replied, "Well, nobody ever told me *not* to do it!"

SEVEN

It was a warm summer afternoon with a hint of rain in the air. Atlee quickened his steps as dark clouds drifted overhead. He had been at the hardware store in Berlin and was walking home to Bunker Hill. As he reached the bottom of the small valley between the two towns, he heard the rattle of steel-rimmed wheels and the hoofbeats of a rapidly approaching horse. He glanced over his shoulder and smiled. The on-coming road cart carried "Rover" John and his wife.

Atlee had worked for John the year before and had enjoyed his time on that farm. One of the memories he had was of a workhorse that John owned. It would peer into the sky and watch an airplane fly overhead. It was the only horse that Atlee had ever seen do that.

"Looks like rain; you better hop on," shouted John as they passed. Atlee ran out behind the cart, grabbed onto the seat frame, and stepped up onto the back.

"Hey, it's been a while since I've had a ride with Rover," said Atlee with a laugh, and John grinned. John's wife turned and glared at Atlee.

"What is the matter with you?" she snapped. "His name is *not* Rover. His name is John, and you need to show some respect!" She continued to chastise Atlee for the remainder of the short ride to the top of the hill.

Atlee stepped off the cart as John slowed the horse and gave Atlee a wink and a wave. Atlee watched the departing cart for a moment, then called out, "Thanks for the ride, **Rover**!"

It was three days before Christmas, 1943, and classes were drawing to a close at South Bunker

Hill School. As Mrs. Spelman stood to dismiss the students, she looked around the room.

"Atlee, I would like for you to stay a few minutes, please."

Atlee gulped. What had he done to get into trouble?

"Okay, Mrs. Spelman."

He sat in his seat and waited as the rest of the students filed out the door. His heart thumped in his chest. He was living with his parents in Bunker Hill, and this was the first year he had Mrs. Spelman as his teacher. Why did she want him to stay? He couldn't remember any misbehavior, and she didn't appear to be upset.

As the last of the students ran off the schoolyard, she sat down at her desk and motioned to Atlee.

"Come up here, please."

She smiled as he shuffled forward.

"Don't worry, you haven't done anything wrong. It's just that I've planned a little surprise for the whole school tomorrow, and I need your help."

Atlee felt a sigh of relief escape his lips as he leaned against the desk. Mrs. Spelman reached into the cabinet behind her and pulled out a faded tweed satchel.

"I have a special Christmas story I'm going to read," Mrs. Spelman continued. "After I've finished the story, I have candy canes I want you to pass out to the other children for me. And..." her smile widened, "I want you to dress up as Santa Claus!"

She pushed the satchel to him across the desk.

"This is my father's Santa suit. He would always dress up as Santa for our family Christmas get-togethers. It might be a bit large for you, but I think you can make do."

A grin spread across Atlee's face as Mrs. Spelman continued her instructions. This was going to be fun! As he headed out the door to go home, Mrs. Spelman called after him.

"Now be sure to not tell anyone! We don't want to spoil the surprise."

That evening and the next morning passed slowly. It was difficult for Atlee to be quiet about the coming surprise. A special treat such as this was rare at school, and the fact that he got to be involved was a high honor.

Atlee had let his mother in on the secret, and in the morning, she delayed his departure for school with an additional chore. After his sister and brothers were gone, Atlee eagerly pulled the suit from the satchel. There was a well-worn red jacket trimmed with white fur, a pair of red pants, and a jaunty Santa hat. It was, as Mrs. Spelman had said, a bit large, but with his mother's help, Atlee was finally ready to be Santa Claus.

Almost ready to head out the door, he remembered Mrs. Spelman's instructions.

"Rub a bit of soot on your face so it appears as though you have been in someone's chimney."

Atlee pulled a piece of charred wood from the stove. Blackening his hands with the soot, he enthusiastically rubbed them over his face. If it was soot she wanted, then soot she would get! He then waited a few minutes before heading to school; he had to coordinate his arrival with Mrs. Spelman's part of the plan.

Meanwhile, at school, the morning's preliminaries were completed and the students settled into their seats for the first class. Mrs. Spelman rose from her chair and clasped her hands.

"Children, it's almost Christmas, and we're going to change our schedule a bit today. I have a story that I would like to read to you."

The children exchanged happy glances as they relaxed in their seats. Mrs. Spelman cleared her throat and began reading *Mr. Bluff's Experience of the Holidays* by Oliver Bell Bunce.

" 'I hate the holidays,' said Bachelor Bluff to me, with some little irritation... "

It was a short story, and Mrs. Spelman soon finished, closed the book, and smiled at the class.

"Now I hope you see that Christmas is about helping others and not just getting things for ourselves. We will now sing a few carols."

Atlee arrived at school and stepped into the wood shed. He waited until he heard the second carol begin, then, easing out the door, he dashed to the corner of the schoolhouse. Mrs. Spelman had suggested that he circle the schoolhouse and peer in the windows. He snuck a peek in the first window. Everyone was singing heartily and didn't notice him. He waited until they came to end of a verse and then lightly tapped on the window. A few of the children turned to look, and Atlee heard a startled shriek.

"Mrs. Spelman, look!"

Every head turned his way as he moved into full view. This was great! He jumped up and down, waving his arms, then ran to the next window. All eyes were on him, and nobody noticed the knowing smile on Mrs. Spelman's face.

Atlee continued his round of the building, knocking on the windows. Where they were covered with wire to stop wayward softballs, he tugged on the wire and pretended to climb up. The students greeted his performance with screams and laughter and, as he opened the door and bounded into the classroom, a few frightened faces.

The normally quiet schoolroom filled with shouts of laughter as Atlee capered up and down between the desks, shouting "Ho ho ho, Merry Christmas!" Spotting an empty seat beside his brother Raymond, Atlee scooted in beside him. The shocked look on Raymond's face told Atlee that Raymond didn't recognize him.

The hilarity continued for several more minutes as Atlee entertained his classmates, but the room quieted as Mrs. Spelman summoned him to her desk and handed him the candy canes. Happy smiles wreathed each face as Atlee—with soot-blackened hands—passed out the treat. There were still a few lessons to be finished, but on that afternoon, the children went home with memories of carols, a Christmas story, and a pint-sized Santa Claus passing out candy canes.

EIGHT

Atlee was fourteen years old and helping "Apple Butter" John make hay. It had been cut, raked, and dried, and John and Atlee harnessed up the team to load it and bring it to the barn. Atlee enjoyed working for John, and he loved driving this strawberry roan team. Responsive and well-trained, these horses were a pleasure to drive.

Atlee drove the horses. John forked the hay evenly onto the wagon as the mechanical loader dumped it onto the back of the wagon. It was hot, dusty work, and they took numerous breaks to rest the horses.

At noon, they took a quick lunch and a short rest, and then headed back to the field. They had scarcely commenced loading when suddenly Colonel, one of the horses, balked.

"Oh c'mon!" Atlee slapped the reins on the horses' broad backs. Colonel refused to move forward, attempting to back up as the other horse patiently stood its ground.

"What's the matter with you? We've got work to do!" Atlee continued to talk patiently to the horses as he attempted to get them moving again. After a few minutes of Atlee's cajoling, Colonel calmed down and leaned into the harness. Having watched the entire incident from atop the tall stack of hay, John laughed.

"Atlee, someday you're going to make a mighty fine preacher!" Neither one of them could have imagined how prophetic those words were.

Atlee's love of fast horses got him into a bit of trouble at times. One Sunday evening, at age fifteen, he was at a singing. Afterwards, a young woman who lived close to his home asked him for a ride home, and he willingly obliged. As they started down the road, they heard the drumbeat of hooves and the rattle of buggy wheels behind them. Two of his friends pulled up alongside.

"Hey, Atlee, how fast can that old nag run?" shouted one of them, and the race was on. Side-by-side down the road they flew, buggy tops swaying, gravel flying from pounding hooves. Atlee's horse was blind, but fast. Atlee was so caught up in the excitement of the action that he never noticed the frightened look on his passenger's face or her white-knuckled grip on the buggy frame.

Atlee was on the right side of the road, his wheels running just along the edge, when he saw a small concrete abutment jutting out from underneath the road into the ditch. He pulled sharply on the left rein, but too late—a sharp jolt, a splintering crash, and the right front corner of the buggy sagged as the wheel shattered.

With the broken spokes of the wheel scraping the dirt, he brought his horse to a halt and got off to survey the damage. This evening's drive was over. He helped his shaken but unharmed passenger off the buggy and asked his friends to take her home. Then, unhitching his horse, he pulled the buggy to the side of the road and began the five-mile walk home.

It was a warm summer night in 1945. The house was silent save for muffled footsteps and the squeak of stair treads as Atlee and his two friends, Bill and Elmer*, descended from the second story. They had spent some time with friends at this home, and now they planned to do a bit more wandering around, as young Amish boys were prone to do on Saturday nights.

They headed for the back door, led by a slender beam of light as Atlee cupped his hand over his flashlight. He paused and held up his hand.

"What is it?" whispered Bill. Silence was essential. Their friends' parents, John and Lavina*, were in a bedroom on the main floor.

"Didn't Edna* say they're having church tomorrow, and her mom baked some pies?" Atlee asked. "Where could they be?"

In the faint light from the flashlight, Atlee could see grins stretch across his friends' faces.

"She probably put them in the basement to cool; that's what my mom does," suggested Bill.

Quietly the boys headed for the basement door and held their breath as the hinges creaked loudly. As Elmer closed the door behind them, Atlee shone his flashlight down the stairway. There were the pies, lined up on shelves built against the wall, their delicate latticework crusts bulging with fruit.

The boys snatched a pie and left through the basement door. Finding no need to go too far before enjoying their ill-gotten gains, they headed for the bank barn behind the house. They entered the lower level and found themselves by the horse stalls.

"We better not eat here," said Bill. "Let's go up to the haymow. If John comes out here, this will be the first place he'll look."

Careful not to drop the pie, Bill led the way up the ladder to the haymow. The large doors at the back of the barn were open, and the dark spread of trees stood in silhouette against dim starlight. Sitting on bales of hay, the boys cut generous slices of pie with their pocketknives. The sweet fruit dripped between their fingers as they savored each mouthful.

Only a few minutes had passed when Elmer stiffened.

"Do you guys hear that?"

No sooner had he spoken than the figure of a man loomed around the large post close beside them. Caught in the act! They had been so enjoying the pie—and impressed by their own cleverness—

that they hadn't heard John coming up the ladder.

The boys leaped to their feet, pie tumbling into the hay, and made a mad dash for the open door. Unfortunately, that meant running directly towards John, who they correctly surmised was not in a good mood. He stepped into Atlee's path and swung his fist as Atlee did a quick side step. Ducking his head, Atlee felt the *whiff* of air as John's fist knocked off his hat. With the loss of his hat being his least concern, Atlee ran for the door.

Almost to safety, he discovered the hard way that, in the shadowy darkness of the barn, he had failed to see a pile of posts stacked just inside the doorway. A sharp pain shot through his leg as he collided with the post pile, and the wind was knocked out of him. He staggered back, then recovered sufficiently to dash out the door. Running for the trees, Atlee saw both Bill and Elmer heading in the same direction as John hurled dire threats from the doorway.

They regrouped in the safety of the woods.

"Are you guys okay?" asked Elmer.

"Man, that was close!" Bill grinned as he wiped his still-sticky hands on his pant leg. "Atlee, I thought you weren't going to make it outta there when those posts got you."

Atlee winced as he rubbed his leg, then reached into his pocket and pulled out his watch. The crystal was cracked, and the hands stood still. He shook his head.

"Well, at least I'll know exactly what time **that** happened!"

They laughed as Atlee told them of his narrow escape from John's fist and that he had lost his hat. They circled through the woods to the road and went home. They had had enough excitement for one night.

Sunday came and went, and Atlee spent most of the day resting. With his leg and ribs still sore, there wasn't much point in a lot of activity.

On Monday morning, as Atlee walked into the kitchen for breakfast after finishing his chores, his father said, "Hey, when you're done with breakfast, we're going to Jake's* to help with the threshing."

Atlee stopped in his tracks. Jake's farm was just down the road from John's place. Chances were good that John was going to be at the threshing. What if John had recognized him in the dark barn on Saturday night or had asked his daughters who their visitors had been? There was no way of knowing, and there was no way of getting out of going to Jake's. When Dad said go, you went.

With breakfast and chores finished, Atlee and his dad headed to Jake's farm. Other neighbors were there to help, and as Atlee entered the barn, he saw John was there, too. Atlee tried to stay as far away from him as possible, and the hours passed as the laborious task of threshing was carried out.

The threshing was almost done when Atlee became aware of someone walking up behind him. He turned and there stood John, his face showing displeasure. There was a moment of tense silence, and then John said, "Well, Atlee, if you want your hat, you'll need to come by the house sometime." He turned on his heel and walked away, leaving Atlee speechless. The afternoon dragged by, and there was no further communication.

It was a lesson Atlee never forgot: No matter how clever you think you are, or how "innocent" the wrong, it doesn't pay to take what's not your own.

He also bought a new hat.

Names have been changed.

Atlee was fifteen years old, and one Sunday at church, he noticed the Swartzentruber boys' sister Mary sitting with the girls, facing the boys.

Chapter Eight

Mary's mother Mandy

Mary's father Andy

Cassimer & Christina Lye
Mary's Great Grandparents

Andy and Mandy

Mary's childhood home

Atlee and Mary at Myer's Lake
c. 1946

She was smiling.

Atlee had never paid too much attention to Mary. He hadn't had that much interest in girls, and besides, she was just his friends' little sister. But that Sunday, he became aware that Mary really was quite cute. That quiet girl he frequently saw standing by the wood-fired cook stove, behind the reservoir, was worth paying some more attention to.

Was she smiling at him? He glanced at Ammon, who was sitting next to him, and saw that no, Mary hadn't been looking at him. Ammon was the recipient of her smile. Atlee was disappointed. Why wasn't she smiling at him?

A few weeks later at a Sunday evening singing, Atlee asked Mary if he could take her home. Much to his disappointment, she already had a ride.

Having faced quite a few challenges in life already, Atlee wasn't about to give up. Although Mary had been dating another boy off and on, Atlee persisted, and soon they began dating. They began a relationship with no idea of what the future held, and a love was born that has lasted a lifetime.

NINE

Atlee treasured the closeness and camaraderie he experienced while spending time with Mary's family. The circumstances of life in his own family did not contribute to such an atmosphere. When Atlee's friendship first developed with the Swartzentruber brothers, neither he nor Mary had any idea that they, too, would be forging a lifetime together.

Although the Barkmans were quite different from Mary's family, the Swartzentrubers, in many ways, they also had much in common. For one thing, they both descended from ancestors who had come from Germany to the United States to build a new life.

Peter Barkman, Atlee's great-grandfather, was born on July 23, 1846, in Rathskirchen, Pfalz, Germany, and came to the United States at age seven, possibly as a stowaway. His brother Daniel is believed to have come at the same time. Not much is known about Peter and Daniel in the first decade after their arrival in the U.S. Their mother and stepfather joined them later.

Daniel enlisted in Captain Allen's Company, 19th Regiment, Ohio Volunteer Infantry, at Berlin, Ohio, on September 7, 1861. He is reported to have said the soldiers rode on open-slatted-side rail cars on their way to Chattanooga, Tennessee, with men on top of the cars and hanging onto the side because they were so crowded. It is believed that he fought at Missionary Ridge on Lookout Mountain, Tennessee, and in numerous other engagements. His obituary states, "...he served for four years and was discharged in 1865 from this service."[1]

Peter married Phoebe Sommers, and they had one daughter, Amanda. Phoebe passed away on January 16, 1872, and is buried in the Walnut Creek

Mennonite Church graveyard. Peter was Lutheran, but after Phoebe's death he joined the Amish, married Rachel Yoder, and moved to Pennsylvania. Peter and Rachel had twelve children. Rachel died in 1897 during the birth of their twelfth child, who also passed away, and they both were buried in the same grave. Peter moved to Geauga County, Ohio, where he married Catherine Weaver, and they later moved back to Holmes County.

Peter was known as a fun-loving guy. He was quite strong, and he would hold a spike in his teeth and bend it. He used to tease the children by hooking them with his cane.

Peter's son Daniel was born in 1875. Daniel was a preacher and then a bishop in the Amish church. Daniel's son John, Atlee's father, was born on June 7, 1901, at the Dan Barkman farm close to the old Farmerstown cheese house.

John Barkman worked for a time at the Sugarcreek brickyard. He later worked at Heini's Cheese in Bunker Hill for fourteen years, for both Crist and John Dauwalder. John Dauwalder's son Pete stated that John Barkman taught him how to brew beer. Pete said it was the only beer that never gave him a headache.

Peter Barkman passed away in 1927 at eighty-one years of age, three years before his great-grand-son Atlee was born on March 30, 1930.

Atlee's mother, Elizabeth (Lizzie), was born on the farm east of what was known as the Plains crossroad, the intersection of County Road 201 and Township Road 207. Atlee later worked on this farm for Yost Miller, who was married to At-lee's aunt. By then, his maternal grandparents, Jake 'Mony' (Emmanuel) and Mattie Miller, lived there in the 'daudy' house. His grandpa was blind, and Atlee remembered seeing him walking out to the barn using his white cane. He was a preacher in the Amish church.

Mary's great-grandparents, Cassimer and Christina Lye, also emigrated from Germany to the United States in the 1850s. In Germany, Cassimer had been a member of the Kaiser's military band. After arriving and settling in the area of Coshocton, Ohio, they found themselves unable to care for all of their children, so several of them were sent to live on neighboring farms.

One daughter, Catherine, lived with an Amish family. After several years there, she met a young man named Simon Swartzentruber. Catherine joined the Amish church, and she and Simon were married.

Simon (Simmy Daudy) lived to be in his nineties. He became a member of the Swartzentruber Amish church, but Catherine did not join him. They are buried in separate cemeteries.

One of Simon and Catherine's sons, Andrew, married a young lady named Amanda Wengerd, whose home was on the north side of Weaver Ridge Road east of Bunker Hill. This farm lay at the intersection of County Road 168 and Township Road 401. The property—which later became the Rolling Ridge Animal Farm—was owned by her parents, Cornelius (Neal) and Mary Wengerd.

Andrew and Amanda (Andy and Mandy) were married on February 3, 1922. Because Simon Swartzentruber had joined a more conservative sect of Amish, he did not attend his son's wedding. Andy's mother, Catherine, did attend. Late in the evening, she headed home with her brother Jonas. Somewhere along County Road 77, north of Township Road 207 between Bunker Hill and Mt. Hope, she became ill. Jonas stopped the horse and helped her off the buggy. She sat on the bank by the side of the road for several minutes, then suddenly slumped over and died, presumably of a heart attack.

After their wedding, Andy and Mandy lived in a small house on the Richardson farm on Township Road 601, approximately three miles from Fredericksburg. Andy worked there for some time, then, a few years before Mary was born, they moved to another farm one-half mile south across the fields, located on Township Road 602. The quarter-mile-long driveway ran south off the road along the east edge of a broad ridge, with the buildings on the rim of the ridge as the fields dropped to the east and south.

Mary was born on this farm July 13, 1931. It was a pleasant place to be a child, with its panorama of wooded hills falling away from the crest of the ridge. Wind was almost a constant, refreshing during the summer but deepening the chill of winter.

Mary at her childhood home

William Kerr purchased the farm around 1936, and Andy and Mandy moved their family a scant quarter mile down the road. They bought a house in Holmesville and moved it to the land they purchased. Splitting the building in half, they remodeled both halves into single-family homes. Andy and Mandy moved their family into one house while Andy's brother Dan and his family lived in the other house. After a few years, Dan moved his family to what was later the Gideon Weaver farm, and their house on Andy's property was torn down.

Andy and Dan dug and slaked limestone for a number of years. They dug the limestone from the eastern slope of the ridge on which they lived, and fired it in the kiln. Heated to approximately 1,000 degrees, these rocks were then loaded onto a cart and wheeled, on a small track, to an area where they were unloaded and sprayed with water. The cold water on the hot rocks caused them to shatter, flake, and turn to a powder, which was then run through a sieve to remove any lumps. This hot, labor-intensive endeavor produced a very effective fertilizer. One customer came all the way from Coshocton, which was quite a trip in those days. There was a long-standing joke in the family about that area being called "Lime City."

As a young girl, Mary did housework for the Kerr family. She specifically remembers washing a lot of dishes. Mrs. Kerr—who was also named Mary—had never learned much about housekeeping; her

Mary and her brother Joe

mother had died when she was young. Mary enjoyed working for her, though, and they got along well.

Mary's mom was well known for her special candy that she made to sell. Caramels, chocolate drops, and peanut brittle were only a few of the creations that she whipped up on her wood-fired stove. Some folks knew her as "Candy Mandy."

Andy worked at Fredericksburg Pottery for more than ten years. Most of the time, he walked the three miles to work. He was a short, slender man, but strong. There were times when, after completing his shift, he would help unload a railway car of supplies for the factory, and then walk those three miles home.

As a teenager, Mary enjoyed riding horses, and would often do so with one of the neighbor girls, Florence. Mary remembers going with her dad to pick up their first buggy with a top. They bought it from Charley Wilson. One of her most treasured memories is of going with her mom to visit her grandma on the Weaver Ridge farm. In the summertime, a favorite snack was sprigs of rue with buttered bread. Coffee was a given, of course, no matter the weather.

---

1. *Barkman: Daniel and Peter: 1750–1978*

TEN

After Atlee and Mary had been dating for a while, another young man attempted to win Mary's heart. He had asked her out a few times and was convinced that she would favor him over Atlee. Thus emboldened, he issued a challenge of sorts to Atlee. Late one evening he came to the farm north of Holmesville where Atlee was working and said, "Hey, listen here. You need to come with me right now! We're going down to Mary's place, and she's going to decide which one of us she really wants." Atlee obligingly got in the buggy and they took the long ride to Mary's house.

Upon their arrival at Mary's home, the young man threw dry corn kernels at her window, and when she opened it, he whispered, "We're here; c'mon out!"

Mary quietly came out the side door and down to the hitching rail. After separately engaging each young man in earnest conversation, she made the decision to continue dating Atlee. The other young man got into his buggy without a word and drove away, leaving Atlee to find his own way home before morning chore time.

One night Mary had a date with a young man named Jimmy.* A bit perturbed, Atlee enlisted the

Atlee and Mary on the right

help of another young man, Will*, and they un-hitched Jimmy's horse and let it run. Then they took Jimmy's buggy through the field and pushed it into the ditch.

Upon returning to his home, Will found that Andy*, a friend of his, was there on a date with Will's sister. Will told Andy what he and Atlee had done.

The next evening, Atlee and Mary had been to visit Atlee's parents, and as they were coming up the road out of the woods close to Mary's home, they saw an oncoming buggy. Atlee had really bright lights on his buggy, and when he turned them on, the other buggy turned around and headed the other way, which raised his suspicions. It was Andy, Jimmy, and Will.

Atlee and Mary continued to her home and went into the house. The three young men headed north over the hill, then circled around through farm lanes and fields and approached the house from the west. They tied their horse a short distance up the road and snuck down to the Swartzentrubers' barn.

Atlee and Ammon, Mary's brother, were watching for them and saw the three young men jump over the ditch by the corner of the barn. Ammon wanted to untie their horse, but after a quick discussion, he and Atlee went out and confronted them instead. Mary also came out and talked to them, as did her father. A situation that could have evoked animosity and spite ended peacefully.

Names have been changed.

It was a breezy Sunday afternoon, and Mary sat on the porch step, reading. Her parents were taking a nap, and her brothers and sister were off on their own pursuits. It was a fine day to relax with a good book. The silence of a peaceful day of rest was broken only by the buzz of insects, the twittering of birds, and the occasional *moo* of a bored cow.

Mary leaned against the railing and her eyes closed momentarily. She had just considered a nap when the growl of a distant motor drifted up the hollow. She sat upright and listened intently. The growl turned into a rumble, accompanied by the cadence of shifting gears. A faint smile crossed her face as she closed her book and stood up. Wrapping her arm around the porch post, she leaned over the railing and gazed across the pasture to where the narrow gravel road twisted up and out of the heavily wooded valley.

The rumble grew louder, and a figure on a motorcycle emerged from the trees, trailed by a plume of dust. Mary descended the steps and skipped down the steep front yard to the hitching pole, a single iron ring nailed to a massive tree stump.

The motorcycle turned onto the small dirt road that ran by the house, the rider manipulating the hand shift and "suicide" clutch with the ease of frequent use. Mary waved, and a smile spread across Atlee's face as he approached. This wasn't the first time he had shown up on his friend's old Indian motorcycle. He pulled up in front of her, dropped the kickstand, and shut off the noisy machine. Shading his eyes with his hand, he grinned up at her.

"It's a nice day. Wanna go for a ride?"

"Sure, just give me a minute to get ready!" Mary ran into the house and returned a few minutes later, dressed more appropriately for the ride. For Atlee and Mary, being dressed appropriately for a motorcycle ride did not include helmets.

It was a beautiful day for a road trip. With no need to hurry, Atlee kept the speed low as they wound their way through the lush countryside. Uphill and down they rolled, past sun-splashed meadows and under towering trees, alongside rippling streams and through Sunday-still villages.

Approaching an intersection, they rolled to a stop. A car passed by, raising a cloud of dust. From the right came a buggy carrying an Amish family. Always one for a bit of flair, Atlee glanced over his shoulder at Mary, winked, and said, "Hang on!"

She wrapped her arms around his waist as a shiver ran up her spine. What was he going to do now?

Revving the engine, Atlee popped the clutch and turned left into the intersection. Gravel flew from under the back tire as they leaned into the corner, and suddenly, they were leaning too far. Mary reached down to brace herself as the motorcycle tumbled to the ground, and stones bit into her hand as she slid along the roadway. Atlee kept his grip on the handlebars as they went down, his knee taking the brunt of the impact. There was a moment of stunned silence as the dust swirled around them, then Atlee said, "Mary, are you okay?!"

"I think so..." Her voice trembled. Getting to her feet, she brushed the dirt from her stinging hands. Atlee still lay on the road, pushing at the bike as he slowly pulled his leg from underneath it.

"Atlee, are you hurt?" Leaning on the handlebar, Atlee pushed himself to his feet. His pant leg, already stained with blood, hung ripped and ragged at his knee. Mary put her arm around his shoulders as he propped his foot up on the bike to take a closer look at his knee. They both focused on the injury, not wishing to look at the occupants of the buggy as it rattled past.

Atlee's knee had a deep scrape (the scar remained for the rest of his life) but neither one was seriously injured. They got the motorcycle back on its wheels and, with the tranquil mood ruined, returned to Mary's home, where they cleaned up, and bandaged Atlee's knee. They spent the rest of the afternoon relaxing on the front porch, thankful that the only damage was to their pride, and Atlee's knee.

One day Atlee had been riding his friend's motorcycle and came home to find that one of his brothers had wrecked his bicycle. He was quite upset that no one would admit to the act, so he decided that a good scare might teach them a lesson. He offered to give each of them a ride on the motorcycle. They eagerly accepted the offer, and he then proceeded to take them on a high-speed (and reckless) ride. He rounded corners so fast and sharp that the floorboard scraped on the road. He achieved his goal of frightening them, but not of extracting a confession.

ELEVEN

In the spring of 1946, at age sixteen, Atlee went to work for a farmer named Dwight Dunham (Atlee, for the rest of his life, simply called him "Dunham".) On this farm north of Holmesville, they used both horses and a Farmall H tractor. While Atlee always liked farming with horses, he also enjoyed using the mechanized equipment on the farm.

Dunham and Atlee did custom work for other farmers in the area. When harvest time came around, they fitted the Farmall H with a two-row corn picker and traveled from farm to farm. Atlee recalls the time they passed Mary's home on the way to the Kerr farm on top of the hill. He was far more interested in trying to see if she was home than in driving the tractor!

The farmers in the neighborhood would help each other fill silos, and sometimes after finishing their work, they would have a little fun. Atlee and the neighbor's hired hand would hook their tractors together and have a pulling contest. Atlee usually won; he drove the Farmall H while the neighbor's hired man had a small Ford. The front wheels of the Ford would lift off the ground as the pulling started, so an onlooker—usually a really big guy—sat on the Ford's front end to hold it down.

Dunham had an old Model A Ford, a dilapidated vehicle that had been reduced to little more than a frame, motor, and seats. He had, at one point, poured concrete into the back for more weight. He called it a "hoopie," and they used it to pull wagons and various farm implements. Dunham had wired chains onto the tires for better traction in the fields, so it wasn't much good for road use. One evening, though, Atlee decided that he wanted to go to Fredericksburg. Clipping the wires, he removed the chains from the tires and, holding a buggy lantern out the side for illumination, drove into town.

Then there was the time Atlee took the hoopie to the neighbors' on an errand, and took one of Dunham's sons with him. When they returned, Dunham informed Atlee that if he didn't slow down, the boys could no longer ride with him.

It was while he was working at the Dunham farm that Atlee bought his first car. It was a Ford with a suitcase trunk, possibly a '49 model. Atlee's friend Sam had a nice Mercury, and they traded cars for a while.

One morning while traveling between Holmesville and Millersburg in Atlee's Ford, Sam was unable to roll down the window to spit, so he opened the door instead. He didn't pay attention to his driving and drove right into the swamp. Two Raymond Patterson Sawmill trucks came by, and the drivers, seeing the car in the swamp, stopped to help. They hooked both trucks to the car and pulled it out, and Atlee's Ford was taken to a garage in Millersburg.

A few days later, Atlee went to the garage to get a pair of boots out of the car, and that was the last time he saw his Ford. He never did find out what happened to it after that—but Sam took back his Mercury.

In later years, Atlee also owned a '56 Chevy, a '52 Mercury, and two Corvairs. Mary's brother Ammon had the distinction of owning a Terraplane, which Atlee said looked like an upside-down bathtub.

Wednesday, October 6, 1948. Atlee hurriedly slung a shovelful of corn into the corncrib. The scrape of the shovel and the thump of corn against the walls of the crib were a common enough noise, but today he found them annoying. Anything that interfered with the voice spilling from the radio was definitely not welcome. The Cleveland Indians were contesting the World Series with the Boston Braves.

It was the first World Series to be shown on a nationwide television network, but television sets were few and far between in Holmes County at the time. Radio was the primary means by which most of rural America had access to the games.

With Indians' pitcher Bob Feller, the "Heater from Van Meter," facing off against Johnny Sain of the Braves, the tension was palpable. In his mind, Atlee could almost picture the scene of more than forty thousand fans in the open-air, horseshoe-shaped stadium, with vendors hustling up and down the aisles selling hot dogs and fifteen-cent Cokes. The excitement was at fever pitch.

After a few more minutes of shoveling, Atlee walked over to the radio. Removing his hat, he ran his hand nervously through his hair. He could almost hear the *crack* of the bat as Phil Masi of the Braves got a hit off of Feller's pitch. And then Masi was out at second base! But wait... the ump called him safe? Over the radio, Atlee could hear a rumble rise from the crowd. They were sure Masi was out. But no, it was the ump's call, and Masi scored the only run of the game, giving the Braves the first win of the Series.

Atlee continued following the games as they progressed. The Braves won the first game, the Indians won the next three, and then came Game 5 in Cleveland.

Cleveland fans expected a win, and a record World Series crowd showed up. The massive stadium overflowed with 86,288 eager devotees. Atlee and his friends gathered around the radio, ready to celebrate the win. Unfortunately for Cleveland fans, Boston showed up with a vengeance and won the game, 11-5.

Another baseball first occurred in Game 5 as Satchel Paige pitched three-quarters of the seventh inning for the Indians. He was the first black pitcher to take the mound in World Series history, and at age forty-two, the oldest Major League rookie.

Game 6. Pitching for the third time in six days, Bob Lemon started for Cleveland and struggled through 7-1/3 innings, giving up three runs on eight hits and four walks before Bearden came on to get the final five outs. Cleveland won the game 4-3, clinching the Series and bringing much joy to Atlee and his baseball-fan friends.

While Atlee always enjoyed hearing of the Tribe's successes, his enthusiasm waned over the years. This was most likely a good thing, as the '48 Series win would be the last one the Indians have had to date.

TWELVE

Atlee brushed a bit of straw off his shirt as he crossed the yard from the barn to the house. He glanced down the long driveway. Dunham and his wife, Dorothy, had gone to town, and Atlee hoped to be gone before they returned. Climbing the stairway to his room, he placed his jacket beside the suitcase that lay on the bed. He walked to the window, but didn't notice the bright sunshine or the leaves of the oak tree fluttering in the breeze. The thought of Mary flashed through his mind, and he shook his head. He should have told her, but there just wasn't time. It had all happened so fast...

Today he would join the National Guard.

The day before, on an errand at the hardware store, he had encountered two of his friends. He didn't get to see much of Irvin and John, and as they talked, he learned that they were planning to join the military. A few years earlier, Atlee's brother Bert had joined the Army Air Corps. While the thought of doing the same had crossed Atlee's mind, he had never given it serious consideration. As his buddies told him of their plans, however, the idea took on a new appeal. They invited him to join them. Hey, why not? It would be an adventure.

As Atlee stood by the window, his stomach tightened with excitement. This would be a big step for him. There was also an unease, however, a deep-seated sense that this might not be the thing to do. He had always been taught that this was wrong, and he had seen his mother's grief when Bert left for the service. But the decision was made, and so he waited with eager anticipation for the crunch of tires on gravel that would signal his friends' arrival.

The appointed time came and went, but they didn't show up. Atlee went to the barn and oiled some of the machinery. If Dunham came home and found him waiting in the house, there would be some explaining to do. Every few minutes he walked over and looked out the barn door. Those minutes grew into hours, and it finally dawned on him that they were not going to come at all.

He did the evening chores, then unpacked his bag and went to bed. His mind was in a whirl. What had gone wrong? He finally fell asleep.

The next day, life on the farm commenced as usual. He never mentioned anything to Dunham, and it would be quite some time before he discovered that his friends simply forgot him on that day. It was a great disappointment at the time, but in looking back, Atlee saw it as the hand of God at work in his life.

It was during Atlee's first winter on the Dunham farm that he became sick with measles. His bedroom was upstairs and cold, with the only warmth being that which drifted up the stairway. Dorothy had settled him on the sofa in the living room, close to the fireplace. On this particular day, both Mr. and Mrs. Dunham were gone for the day, and Atlee was lying on the sofa, asleep.

Dunham's mother was staying with them at the

time. She was upstairs, but thinking she smelled smoke, she came downstairs to check. Finding no source of the smell in the kitchen, she entered the living room. Atlee was still asleep on the sofa.

Peering across the room, she saw a tendril of smoke that didn't seem to be coming from the fireplace. She walked over to Atlee and saw that a spark from the fire had landed on the blanket, and a small flame had just sprung up. Grabbing the glass of water that Dorothy had placed by the sofa for the patient, she quickly doused the threat. Atlee was so sick that he was completely unaware of the danger.

One Friday evening, Dunham walked into the barn just as Atlee was finishing up the chores.

"Hey, Atlee, would you and Ervin want to go to a football game in Wooster tonight?"

"Sure!" responded Atlee, and he hurried to the house to clean up. He had never been to a football game. After a quick supper, Dunham and Atlee picked up Ervin—neighbor Clark Taylor's hired hand—and headed for Wooster in Dunham's old maroon Chevy. Arriving at the game, they each got a root beer as they headed to the bleachers, and the game commenced.

It didn't take At-
lee and Ervin long
to realize they didn't
know much about
football and really
didn't care to. Atlee
elbowed Ervin in the
ribs.

Atlee on the left

"I'm going to take
a walk; wanna come
along?" They walked
out to the parking
lot. Atlee laughed as he leaned against the dented fender of a dust-covered Ford. "Well, whaddya
think about football?"

Ervin grimaced.

"Looks like too much running around and getting knocked down for my taste. Let's head downtown and see what's going on."

The young men crossed the parking lot and
strolled down the sidewalk. As they walked along
the busy street, a faded blue Chevy coupe slowly
rolled up beside them and somebody said, "Hey,
what are you guys doing in town tonight?"

Turning, the boys saw Johnny Byler and Bill
Miller, two young men they hadn't seen for quite

some time. The four were casual acquaintances, and so they spent some time catching up on the goings-on in their respective neighborhoods.

"So what are y'all going to do the rest of the evening?" asked Atlee, and Johnny grinned.

"Well, we're just heading out to Indiana for the weekend. Got some friends out there that we're going to look up. You guys want to go along?"

"Sure, why not?"

With Dunham and any later chores forgotten, the boys clambered into the back seat. The first few hours of the drive were full of lively conversation, but Atlee fell asleep close to midnight. Finally, in the early morning hours, they arrived at the home of Bill's friend.

After getting a few hours of sleep and a hearty breakfast, the boys spent the next two days in aimless adventures. There was a ball game, some meeting of old friends and making of new ones, and general mischief. They didn't return to Ohio until Sunday night, with enough time for a bit of sleep before Monday's work began.

Dunham's only comment on Atlee's disappearance was that he had wanted Atlee to unload corn on Saturday.

THIRTEEN

Atlee had lived with numerous families while growing up, so there didn't seem to be a place for him to call home. By the age of eighteen, he was ready to settle down with Mary, so in 1948, both of them joined the Amish church. Wedding plans began in earnest, and they married on December 29, 1949.

There was the frantic activity of preparation, and then the wedding day dawned. The day was cold, with a blustery wind sweeping flurries of snow across frozen fields, but nothing could dampen their love and excitement. The ceremony and reception were held east of Bunker Hill at the home of Mary's grandparents, Neal and Mary Wengerd, on the Weaver Ridge.

Tables for guests had been placed in the living room, the dining room, and the expansive family room. Small cut-glass dishes of pickles and beets were set out, and the smell of chicken and mashed potatoes wafted from the kitchen.

The ceremony came to an end, and the wedding feast was served. Atlee and Mary were seated at the bridal table, along with their four witnesses. The table, covered with a white tablecloth and set with Grandma's heirloom dinnerware, was situated in the corner of the family room. As the meal drew to a close, Mary's sister Nettie brought her son David up to the table. He was just three months old, and the women adored him.

It was a day that opened the door into a new future, a day for family and friends, and it drew to a cold but happy end.

Atlee and Mary did not, however, start their married life as most people do, spending time with and focusing on each other. There was no honeymoon and no time to relax. Mr. and Mrs. Lester Schlabaugh had asked the newlyweds to babysit their children while they went on vacation for a month. So Atlee and Mary began married life by staying in the Schlabaugh home, taking care of eight children and doing the chores. It was quite a challenge for a bride and groom still in their teens. All went well, however, and in a month they were ready to move on.

Atlee had been asked to work for Sam Miller (Mexican Joe's Sam), so the young couple moved in with Mary's parents for a while, and Atlee farmed for Sam throughout the year of 1950.

Although Atlee enjoyed farming with mechanized equipment, his experiences with it were not always positive.

On a cool spring day, Atlee hooked the manure spreader to the tractor and began fertilizing. The farm was on hilly terrain, and he had to be careful as he negotiated the ups and downs of the fields.

Time passed pleasantly enough as Atlee continued his task. As he opened a gate on a hilltop, he looked out across the landscape. The fresh, bright green of spring swept across the rolling countryside, and he paused for a moment to take in the scene. He drove through the gate, then stopped and walked back to close it. Hooking the chain over the post, he turned around just in time to see the tractor and spreader slowly begin to roll down the hill. He made a frantic dash to get to the tractor, but was too late.

Gaining momentum, the tractor careened downhill with the spreader swaying and bouncing behind it, chunks of manure flying through the air. Tractor and wagon smashed through a fence, hurtled down another steep slope, and telescoped into a massive rock jutting up from the ground.

The tractor was damaged beyond repair, so Sam deducted $100 from Atlee's wage to pay for it. After that, Atlee had to use the horses to do the farming.

It was a warm summer evening, and the trees stretched their shadow-fingers across the fields as the sun sank towards the horizon. Gravel rattled under buggy wheels as Atlee and Mary headed down the road.

Bill Detweiler had asked Atlee to come and work for him, so, early in 1951, Atlee and Mary moved into a small house on his farm, about a mile south of Holmesville. Mr. Detweiler had previously kept chickens in that house, and it took a lot of cleaning, but it became their first home.

They called it their chicken coop.

They had been shopping at the Holmesville grocery store and were now headed home. Atlee's brother Emanuel planned to pick them up at home, and they would go to visit Atlee and Emanuel's parents.

Atlee with his horse Ted

With a fast horse named Ted, they weren't concerned about getting home before darkness fell. Ted, knowing that rest and a full feed bin awaited him, quickened his pace as they left Holmesville.

As they topped the rise and started down the last small hill before their driveway, a car horn blared as Emanuel passed them. (He told them later that, according to his speedometer, Ted was traveling at 32 mph.)

"Do you think the others will be there tonight?" wondered Mary. "We haven't seen them for quite a while."

"I don't know," said Atlee. "I guess they've all been pretty busy... Oh no!"

His voice broke off abruptly, and Mary heard a sharp intake of breath.

"What's wrong?" She looked over and saw him staring intently at the horse.

"Look at this!" He gave a sharp tug on the right rein, and it came back freely in his hand. The snap attaching the rein to the bit in the horse's mouth had detached.

The buggy swayed as Ted headed down the hill. He was going home, and there was no holding him back.

They were only a few hundred yards away from their driveway. It wouldn't take long to get there, and Atlee and Mary both knew Ted would take the sharp left turn into the driveway no matter his speed. The buggy would not make it around the corner on all four wheels, and on the far side of the driveway stood a wooden platform for milk cans. The chance of striking that platform was huge, and the likelihood of injury or even death was very real.

The color drained from Mary's face as she gripped the side of the buggy opening.

"Should we jump?"

"No," said Atlee, "we'll just get hurt!" They were rapidly approaching the driveway; he knew he had to do something, and quickly.

There was only one thing to do. He stood up and, swinging his foot over the dashboard, stepped out onto the shaft. Ignoring the roadway rushing by beneath him, he leaned on Ted's back as he worked his way forward. He could feel the animal's powerful muscles rippling and the shaft bouncing beneath his feet as Ted hurtled down the road.

A few quick steps, and he grabbed the horse collar and threw his leg across the horse's back. He leaned hard against Ted's neck as he reached forward, trying to get a grip on the bridle. Ted's head bobbed up and down as he ran, and his mane blew into Atlee's eyes and stung his face. The driveway was fast approaching; there were only seconds to spare. Emanuel, who had glanced in his mirror and seen Atlee astride the horse, now stood in the road by the driveway, waving his arms in a vain attempt to slow Ted down.

Atlee reached forward again, and his hands closed around the bridle just above the bit. He tightened his knees on the horse's shoulders and leaned back with all his strength.

"Whoa, Ted, whoa!"

Ted's neck arched as his head was pulled back, and he broke his stride. Another heave backward by Atlee, and Ted came to a prancing halt right at the end of the driveway. Emanuel ran over and grasped the bridle.

"Hey, are you two all right?"

Atlee released his grip and laughed, albeit a bit shakily.

"I think so."

He slid off Ted's back and walked back to the buggy. Mary said nothing as he helped her step down, but her face was pale and her hands trembled. They were both well aware that, by the grace of God, disaster had been averted by mere moments.

There was always a suspicion that the rein was loosened intentionally, as neither the snap on the rein nor the ring on the bridle was broken.

In the fall of '51, Atlee and Mary purchased land across the road from Mary's parents, Andy and Mandy. They then bought a house below Sugarcreek and had it hauled to their property, a move of almost twenty miles. Wagner Trucking Company did the hauling, and the move cost just sixty dollars. After adding a few additional rooms to the house, they moved in.

Atlee and Mary lived there for the next

thirty-nine years. Living so close to her parents was a tremendous blessing for Mary. She could share so much with her mother: cooking, gardening, and coffee breaks, along with the encouraging conversations that accompanied them.

Mary at home. And yes, that is an 8' Geranium!

FOURTEEN

Atlee's life had always been unsettled, even from childhood. It had continued to be so as he grew into his late teens and dated Mary. He was short, only 5'6", but his quick temper and bravado more than made up for his stature.

His circumstances stabilized somewhat when he and Mary joined the Amish church and were married, but there was still something missing. He had grown up attending the Amish church, but it was mostly a formality. One thing noticeably missing in his life was sound Scriptural instruction. Although he attended church, he gave scant thought to God. He didn't know there could be a personal relationship with Jesus Christ. Life was hard, and frequently, so were the people. Nobody had ever fully explained to him that he had a loving Father in heaven.

Although there was not much knowledge or even an interest in knowing God during those years, Atlee could later plainly see the hand of God at work in his circumstances. The people, the events, and the course of his life at that time were all used by God to shape him into the man he became. He would, for the rest of his life, tear up as he talked about the love and mercy of his heavenly Father.

In 1952, life changed course again. The military draft was in effect at the time, and Atlee received his notice in the mail. He was to report to the draft board in Wooster for an interview. A physical was also required.

A dense fog blanketed the landscape on the morning of the interview, and Atlee's driver didn't show up. The knot in Atlee's stomach tightened as the clock ticked steadily on. Realizing that he could wait no longer if he wanted to make his appointment, he hurried across the field to neighbor George Leiber's house and explained the situation. Fortunately, Mr. Leiber was available to take him, and Atlee arrived at the draft board office with just minutes to spare.

The draft board granted Atlee's request to enter the 1-W program, and upon his passing of the physical, he was to report for service.

The 1-W (conscientious objector) program provided opportunities to work in civil service jobs such as highway construction, at hospitals, or in the national parks. This being a government program, it could be quite confusing to figure out all the details and requirements. "Corn" Crist Miller helped the local Amish boys through the red tape.

Mary's brothers Ammon and Joe had signed up to work at hospitals in Cincinnati, and Atlee was able to serve with them. Atlee and Joe worked at St. Mary's Catholic Hospital, while Ammon was employed at Good Samaritan Hospital.

In April 1952, the three men moved to Cincinnati and stayed at the hospital while looking for a house to rent. Six months later, they located a suitable place not too far from the hospital and moved in.

Atlee was scheduled to be in 1-W service for

two years, so he and Mary rented their house to the Aaron Troyer family during that time. Mary had been staying with her parents until she could join Atlee in Cincinnati.

That day finally came. Atlee and Ammon drove up to Holmes County and loaded her bags into the car. She was excited and a bit apprehensive about a move to the city, but nothing mattered as much as being with Atlee again.

She grew quiet as they drove south into Cincinnati. This was not a quick trip, a one-day visit to town and then home again. This city would be home for the next year and a half.

The car wound its way through the city onto Euclid Street and pulled up in front of a two-story house. It was an older house, but well maintained. There were houses on either side and across the street, but the back yard sloped down to some trees that provided a slight relief from the cityscape.

This move to the city was a culture shock for all of them. Far removed from the peace and quiet of the Amish countryside, they were now in a big city with all the grime, crime, and noise that accompanied it. St. Mary's Hospital was in a less-than-well-to-do neighborhood, and the required adjustment was extreme.

They finally settled into their life in the city. At-lee did maintenance at the hospital, washing walls and painting and working in the greenhouse. While some 1-W workers served as orderlies in hospitals, Atlee was glad to be working in maintenance at St. Mary's. He did not like the noises made by people in pain, or the sound of frozen bodies tossed onto steel gurneys.

Mary stayed at home, cooked, and took care of the house. Those were lonely days for her. It wasn't safe to go walking around by herself, so when her work was done, she found herself sitting by the window, watching city life pass by. On Atlee's days and evenings off, they went out to eat with Ammon and Joe, or walked and explored the city.

One day as they were walking along the river, they passed a small dock where a man was untying his boat.

"Hey, folks, want to go for a ride?"

They hesitated. Why was this stranger offering them a ride? Well, he looked relatively harmless, so they got into the boat. It turned out to be an enjoy-able and informative ride. Their guide took them up and down the river, pointing out sites of interest along the way.

As they approached the docks a few hours later,

they did so with a greater knowledge and appreciation of the Cincinnati riverfront.

One of the more tragic occurrences while Atlee and Mary were in Cincinnati was the death of a young man they had befriended. Jim* was only sixteen or seventeen years old, but already in bad company. Late one evening, he and his friends encountered a few other young men with whom they had previously fought. Tempers flared, insults were exchanged, and fists flew. Jim, trading blows with a member of the other gang, took a solid hit to the face and stumbled back a few steps. He then toppled over backward, striking his head on the curb and dying almost instantly.

Atlee and Mary had become accustomed to the fact that crimes occurred in their neighborhood on an almost daily basis, but Jim's death was a sharp reminder that they were not living in Holmes County anymore.

There were eight young men in the 1-W program: Atlee, Ammon, Joe, Leonard Brunk, Abe Beachy, Alvin Schlabaugh, Lee Schlabaugh, and Aden Troyer. A few of them were married, and there were many good times spent in each other's company when the workday was over.

One day after lunch, Lee approached Atlee.

"Hey, would you and Mary be interested in join-ing us if we started a Sunday School?"

Atlee hesitated. He had never attended Sunday school, and he couldn't imagine it being very inter-esting. He shrugged. What could it hurt?

"So how often are you going to have this Sunday school?"

Lee smiled. He knew Atlee was open to trying new things, so he wasn't too surprised when Atlee considered it.

"Well, it's going to be every Sunday. I think you'll find it interesting. We're going to hold the Sunday school in the Quiet Quakers' meetinghouse, before their service, and they said we're welcome to stay for theirs if we want to. There's also a Bap-tist church close by that we can attend."

So that's how most of the 1-W team spent their Sunday mornings. They had an hour of Sunday school in the balcony of the Quaker meetinghouse, with teaching by various members of the team. A few would then attend the Quaker service, which Atlee and Mary found a bit unsettling. While being accustomed to sitting quietly during a long church service, it seemed strange to have no singing or preaching. The Quakers sat silently throughout the entire service, only speaking up as they felt prompted to do so.

Atlee and Mary also frequently attended the Baptist church. They enjoyed the talented choir and the Biblical preaching.

The 1-W team held weekly Bible studies, and Atlee and Mary began to read their Bible much more than they ever had. They attributed this newfound interest in the Bible to the drawing of the Holy Spirit and, as Atlee said, "My mother's prayers."

Reading his Bible was often the first thing that Atlee did when returning from work, and he found that he would rather read than eat. The power of the Word gripped his heart, and his eyes were opened to the truth of it.

One evening, Atlee read Hebrews 4:12: *For the Word of God is quick, and powerful, and sharper than any two-edged sword, piercing even to the dividing asunder of soul and spirit, and of the joints and marrow, and is a discerner of the thoughts and intents of the heart.*

He walked into the kitchen, where Mary was preparing supper.

"Mary, if we want to go to heaven, we have to live by what this Word says. We can't go by what man says; we have to live by this book." **

It was a life-changing moment for both of them. Believing in Christ and beginning a relationship with a Heavenly Father who truly loved them opened a doorway for Atlee and Mary. They stepped through that door and never looked back. Life took on new meaning and purpose, and they began a journey with God that continued for the rest of their lives.

* Name has been changed.
** See page 204

After Atlee had completed his term of service, they moved back to Holmes County. Atlee did carpentry work during the summer, first with John Miller (known as Long John) and then with George Christner, Mary's brother-in-law.

As winter approached and the carpentry business slowed, he worked at the Fredericksburg Pottery, where he encountered an unusual request by his boss.

The crisp fall breeze curled around the corner of the building and ruffled Atlee's shirt. He paused for a moment to enjoy it as he wiped the sweat from his brow, then tightened his grip on the sledgehammer and raised it above his head.

Another swing, another clay mold shattered.

It was his first day on the job at the Fredericks-burg Pottery, and he had been assigned the task of breaking up the old, worn-out molds. He tackled the job with enthusiasm. It certainly wasn't the hardest he had ever worked, and it was nice to get an hourly wage. He was so engrossed in his job that he didn't notice Chuck, the foreman, coming through the open door at the back of the building. Atlee looked up as the man approached.

"Hey you, what's your name again? Atlee? Listen, Atlee, you need to slow down a bit. These molds don't all have to be busted up in one day, you know!"

The foreman turned and reentered the building, and Atlee stood still for a moment. He was stunned. He had never been told to work more slowly. At every other job he had, the faster you worked, the better the boss liked it. He had never known a farm-er that wanted his hired hands to dawdle, and the nuns at the hospital in Cincinnati did not take kind-ly to anyone who shirked their duties. He resumed his task at a more leisurely pace, and his mind drift-ed back to Cincinnati.

Those two years had brought tremendous change. Newly married, living in the city, and encountering the challenges of a different culture had moved both Atlee and Mary outside of their comfort zone. The most significant change had been entering into a personal relationship with Jesus Christ. That relationship brought joy and a depth of meaning into their lives they had not experienced before.

Surrendering his life to Christ also brought about a change of identity for Atlee. As a young boy and then as a teenager, he was ashamed to be known as John Barkman's son. As a believer in and a follower of Christ, that shame vanished. He came to realize that his identity lay in his heavenly Father's love for him.

Atlee also came to love his dad, and the first thing he wanted to do upon his return from Cincinnati was to share the good news of Christ's love with him. Finding an opportunity one day while they both happened to be in the milk house, Atlee told his dad of the new life to which he had been led. John Barkman was a hard man, but that day he simply listened as Atlee spoke, and the tears ran down his face and dripped onto the milk house floor.

John never made a public acknowledgment of believing in Christ, and his sudden death of a heart attack at age sixty-six was a severe blow for Atlee.

FIFTEEN

Dwight and Dorothy Dunham attended the Methodist church in Fredericksburg. Their son Gale had been a chaplain in the Army, and when he returned, he had the opportunity to preach on a Sunday morning. Mr. and Mrs. Dunham invited Atlee and Mary to attend the service, and after Gale finished his sermon, he asked Atlee to come up and give the closing prayer. That was uncomfortable for Atlee, being a young Amish man.

Although Atlee and Mary had always planned

to remain Amish, some of their views began to change. With great reluctance, they concluded that the Amish church might not be the best fit for them, and they began their search for different fellowship. They started attending Zion Conservative Mennonite Church close to Benton and, in 1960, officially became members of that congregation.

Upon their leaving the Amish church, the bishop paid Atlee and Mary a visit. After a congenial conversation, he told them that because he didn't want to cause them too much trouble, they would not be placed in the *bann*.

Atlee did experience some turmoil during this transition. He just wasn't sure what to do. Up

Atlee and Mary

until that point, he would always whistle as he was out and about, but after making this difficult decision, the whistling stopped. He knew this was the path God wanted for them and he was content in God's will, but the whistling never returned.

Although Atlee and Mary made the decision to leave the Amish church, they always had a high regard for the Amish. They were never ashamed of having been Amish; their respect for and friendship with their family, friends, and the Amish community was never in doubt.

Andy Weaver provided a ride to church for Atlee and Mary because they didn't have a car for quite some time after leaving the Amish church. They also didn't have a phone or electricity for a long time after joining the Mennonites. They finally bought a car, but it was quite a while before they acquired a phone.

After a few years of marriage, they began to wonder if they would ever be blessed with a child. But after seven years, in 1956, their first son, Mervin, arrived. A daughter, Ellen, followed one year later, in 1957. In 1961, Joseph was born, and in 1964, Philip. Another daughter, Naomi, was born in 1969, but her birth was followed by tragic news. The doctors informed Atlee and Mary that Naomi's heart was malformed, and at that time there was no means of repairing it. She lived and was loved for twenty-nine days, and then, on July 6, breathed

Mary holding Laban

her last and slipped into the arms of her Creator. Mary had three miscarriages, one before Merv was born, one between Ellen and Joe, and one between Joe and Phil.

Laban - 8 years old

Laban was born in 1970, and he, too, endured a number of handicaps. He was never capable of speaking. At an early age, he became hydrocephalic, and his doctors placed a shunt in his head to relieve the pressure. He required constant care, and Mary devoted herself to giving him the best quality of life possible. Laban greatly enjoyed attending the Holmes County Training Center and was much loved by the staff there, as well as by his bus driver, Mattie Miller. At age 28, he contracted spinal meningitis, and, despite the best efforts of his doctors, he passed away on July 19, 1998. His family treasured their years with him, and his passing left a hole in Mary's heart that could only be healed by the touch of God.

Late 1960s, Thursday morning, sometime after 2:00 am. The house was dark and quiet; all were asleep. In the southwest corner of the house, Atlee and Mary had their window open to the night breeze that wafted through the leaves of the towering oak outside. Suddenly Mary woke up, too suddenly. What was that noise? It had awakened her but ended before she became fully aware. She lay still, eyes wide open as the darkness pressed in.

There it was again, a low rumble, and goose bumps prickled up as she recognized the sound. She was accustomed to the plaintive *moo* of the average cow in the field, but the agitated grumble of the male of the species sends an entirely different message. And this rumble was close—right under the window of their second-story bedroom.

"Atlee! Atlee, wake up!"

He woke with a start and raised himself on his elbow, just in time to hear the crunch of hooves on gravel and the sharp crash of horn against metal.

"What is going on?" Swinging his feet over the side of the bed, Atlee went to the window. In the driveway, with the dense darkness of the trees just beyond, stood the Dodges, a Coronet and the older Dart. A patch of white moved in front of the Dart, and Atlee's eyes focused on the hulking form of neighbor Emanuel (Mony) Shetler's Hereford bull as it took another stab at the car's grille.

Throwing on his clothes, Atlee dashed down the basement steps, grabbing a shovel as he ran out the door. Scooping up some gravel, he hurled it at the animal. "Go on, get outta here!"

Ignoring Atlee and his shovel, the bull continued its determined attempt to intimidate the unyielding vehicle. After a few more shouts from Atlee, the animal wheeled and eyed him menacingly, then advanced towards him. Atlee beat a quick retreat into the basement and watched through the window as the bull headed along the side of the house toward the sidewalk leading to the front porch.

By this time, the commotion had awakened the children, who were running from window to window, watching the angry animal approach. The porch was a concrete slab about four feet above the ground, and the bull stuck its head over the top. Shaking its horns, it bellowed and threatened, an intimidating sight from the glass sliding door, a bare ten feet in front of it.

After a few heart-stopping moments, the bull left the porch and circled the back of the house at a run, cutting one corner so short that it knocked loose the downspout. It came around the front of the house again and wandered about for a few minutes, finally disappearing into the darkness towards Andy and Mandy's driveway.

But the excitement wasn't over yet. Andy and Mandy had awakened to the sound of Atlee's shouting and the bull's bellowing, and Andy dressed and headed out the door to see what was going on. The porch was on the east side of the house, and as the screen door slammed behind him, Andy took in a deep breath of the damp night air, laced with the faint scent of Mandy's morning glory plant that stretched from railing to roof. He stepped off the stone slab step and rounded the corner of the porch, and there, just a few feet in front of him, was a big, unhappy bull!

Fortunately, Andy reacted faster than did the bull and reversed course onto the porch and into the house in record time.

In the meantime, Atlee drove up to Mony's house to inform him of the situation. As the bull meandered around Andy and Mandy's yard, Mony came down the hill with his dog, a scruffy black and white mix. In spite of his dubious pedigree, Scruffy was quite adept at the herding of bulls, even angry ones. With Mony giving a few terse commands, the dog herded the bull up the hill and back to the barn.

And so ended the night's excitement. With only a few dents in the Dart's grille and a loosened downspout, it all turned out to be a great story to tell.

SIXTEEN

Guatemala, 1976. It was a small airport, but then, it was also a small country. The double doors leading into the terminal were propped open, and Atlee glanced around as he walked in. Sunlight streamed hot through the dirty glass of the windows facing the parking lot, and the two fans circling lazily overhead did little to relieve the oppressive heaviness of the atmosphere. His stomach knotted as he approached the rickety ticket counter. He was in a foreign country for the first time, and the surly man taking his ticket was a far cry from the cheerful lady who had checked his bags in Columbus.

Passport picture of Atlee

"Ticket, identification," grunted the man in heavily accented English, and Atlee handed over his license and the booklet containing the tickets. The man took them and stepped to the table behind him, on which were a number of desktop files. Atlee glanced over his shoulder. Marion Good, the other member of the mission board, had already been processed and was waiting. As Atlee turned to the counter again, the agent approached and handed back the items.

Atlee slid them into his pocket and rejoined Marion. As they headed for the small side room to retrieve their luggage, Marion glanced at Atlee.

"Do you have your ticket for Puerto Rico?"

"Yes, I've got it right here."

"Let me see it."

Puzzled, Atlee pulled the booklet out of his pocket and flipped it open.

"See, right here...." He stopped short as he saw the perforation where the ticket should have been. Marion halted and turned on his heel.

"Come with me." He strode back towards the ticket counter as the agent watched their approach. Marion motioned the agent closer.

"Where is this man's ticket?" he asked, jerking his thumb at Atlee. The agent shrugged and shook his head. Marion leaned his large frame on the counter and scanned the area behind it. Spotting a trash can beside the table, he stabbed his finger at it and said emphatically,

"There! Look in there!"

The agent shook his head again, and a bead of sweat trickled down the side of his face.

Marion, a seasoned traveler, wasn't about to give up.

"You had this man's ticket, and you need to look in that trash can right now!" The agent's eyes shifted around the room. The half-dozen other passengers in line were starting to pay attention now, and two other airport employees behind the counter were watching him.

Slowly he bent over the trash can and rummaged through crumpled papers and the smelly contents of emptied ashtrays. And there was the ticket. Holding it between finger and thumb, the agent brought it over to the counter and handed it to Atlee without a word.

Atlee placed the rescued ticket back in his pocket and they went to get their luggage, only to discover that Atlee's suitcase had not arrived. And so for the next five days, as Atlee and Marion visited with the resident missionaries and preached at the local church, Atlee did so with only one set of clothes.

The trip to Guatemala was not a vacation. Atlee had served in the office of deacon at Zion Conservative Mennonite Church since 1965, received his ordination as a minister in 1973, and was a member of the mission board. He recalled how, the night before he was ordained deacon, he couldn't sleep. At 3:00 am he went into the bathroom, knelt in over the bathtub, and prayed, "Lord, if this is your will, then I'll accept it." He went back to bed, slept for two hours, and when he got up he felt as though he had had a full night's sleep.

Atlee taught Bible school in Carbon Hill, Ohio, during the mid-to-late '60s. He was on the church mission board for years, during which the unpleasant incident in Guatemala took place. For a time, he led the outreach congregation at Oak Hill, southwest of Becks Mill. At various times, Atlee visited Guatemala, Paraguay, Brazil and Costa Rica, mostly to establish or visit missions.

He was also called as an evangelist and traveled extensively throughout the eastern United States and Canada, preaching the Word of God.

These years had brought much change for Atlee and Mary. Along with his service to the church, there was also the responsibility of raising five children, with one being a special needs child. Life was focused primarily on family and church.

Atlee did not have the example of a godly father to follow but he still, by the grace of God, became one. He was the first to admit his mistakes, though, and in later years expressed the regret he felt at being gone from home so frequently during his evangelistic crusades.

While he was quite strict in one sense, home life was happy for the Barkman family. The consistency of Atlee and Mary's walk of faith, both in public and at home, created a stability for the family that Atlee had never experienced.

Vacations were few and far between, but in 1973, the family went to Sarasota, Florida, for two weeks. Atlee had a Dodge Kary Van that he used for work, and it was quite spacious with all his work tools removed. He emptied it out and installed carpet, cabinets, and extra seats, turning it into a camper/motor home of sorts.

Florida was an adventure for the Barkman family. Sarasota was a big city, but then, being in Pinecraft felt strangely familiar; most will recognize it as a sunny, more densely populated microcosm of Holmes County, Ohio. The beach, though, was the primary attraction for the children; sand, seashells, and endless rolling waves beckoned.

The one dark moment was the day that Laban had a seizure. The family was at the beach when it occurred. An elderly man that was witness to it ran to his car to go phone for help. Just as he reached his car, he saw a police car drive through the parking lot, so he began honking his car horn. The police officer noticed the continued blaring and returned. Told of what was happening, he summoned an ambulance and help soon arrived for Laban. He spent a day in the hospital, but recovered fully.

Atlee not only expected that his children respect their mother, but he showed that respect in everyday life. While he had been an angry and foul-mouthed young man, those traits were not to be found in his life after his conversion. He freely shared with friends and family alike how God had removed those vices from him. He would, for the rest of his life, marvel at the fact that God had rescued him from a life of sin.

Another trait that apparently came all the way down from Atlee's great-grandfather Peter was an irrepressible sense of humor. Many evening hours were spent sitting around the supper table long after the meal was over, talking, laughing, and sharing.

Speaking of meals, one of Atlee's favorites was "mush und milich." After making a big batch of mashed potatoes, Mary would tear bread into small chunks, browning it in butter. She would then stir these crispy morsels into the mashed potatoes. Everyone would have a cup half full of cold milk by their plate; the hot mashed potatoes and bread would be scooped up on a spoon, dunked into the cold milk, and enjoyed.

Atlee took the preaching of the Word very seriously, but there were unintended moments of levity. He was an energetic speaker, never known to stand quietly behind the pulpit.

It was a Wednesday evening, and the faithful were streaming into the church house. Atlee was seated in the small meeting room in the basement, sharing thoughts with Eli Yutzy, the pastor of this Minnesota congregation.

Atlee was here for a week of revival meetings, and attendance had been fair both Monday and Tuesday evenings. Tonight promised to be a packed house, as most of the congregation kept their Wednesday nights open for prayer meeting.

After having prayer together, Atlee and Eli seated themselves on the podium as the song leader began the service with a number of hymns. The harmony of praise filled the auditorium. After a brief devotional by an assistant pastor, Atlee stepped up to the pulpit. As he scanned the crowd, the responsibility of his mission rested heavy on his shoulders. To preach the Word of God in truth and love was not only his calling, but also his joy.

It didn't take long for Atlee to get to the heart of his topic. Never known to be a boring or mild-mannered preacher, his enthusiasm was contagious. He paced back and forth on the platform, then paused to read more Scripture. As he enthusiastically pounded the pulpit to make a point, he saw a flash of motion out of the corner of his eye, heard a rattle in the aisle, and saw a piece of molding from the pulpit go bouncing along the floor. As smiles broke out among the congregants, Atlee had to restrain his own laughter.

One privilege of being a pastor was being able to attend the denomination's ministers' meetings. These gatherings were times of hearing the Word, learning more about it, and sharing the successes and failures of leadership. They were also, however, times of relaxation and enjoying good, clean fun. It frequently meant bunking in dorm rooms and sharing meals in communal lunchrooms, which seemed to bring out the boy in these otherwise staid pillars of the church. They played pranks on each other, and one individual's propensity, when startled, to shout out whatever was going through his mind at the moment was a source of great hilarity.

Another incident in which Atlee had to suppress his laughter occurred while preaching in Rome, New York. A member of the congregation had invited a friend to the service, and they sat in the front row. The visiting lady was not a Mennonite and apparently was unfamiliar with the oratory antics of Mennonite preachers, at least this one. Again, Atlee was very involved in his subject and slammed his hand on the pulpit to emphasize his point. Startled, the lady jumped visibly, and Atlee had to go to great pains to hide his amusement.

An occurrence that probably did not amuse Atlee as much as it did his listeners was the time when, making an emphatic point with his hands as well as his words, he knocked his own glasses off his face.

In 1977, Atlee and Mary, along with a few other families, left the Zion church and formed a new congregation called Faith Haven Fellowship, which continues to this day, led by Bishop Tim Miller.

Atlee and Mary

SEVENTEEN

Atlee began working at Holmes Lumber in 1961 and worked there for twenty-seven years. At first, he manufactured and installed kitchen cabinets, working with Roy Wengerd. He also did installation and remodel work, which involved almost every kind of task imaginable. Floor coverings, ceilings, doors and windows, drywall, plumbing, cabinets—if it needed to be done, Atlee was sent to do it. His starting wage was $1.55.

For six years, Atlee worked Monday through

Thursday at Holmes Lumber, then worked with Atlee Miller doing pest extermination on Friday and
Saturday.

Merv, Joe, and Phil all worked with Atlee at
Holmes Lumber in their early teens. Atlee was
quite meticulous, and did his best to teach his sons
to work well. His instructions on how to cut a board
were simple: Make sure your measurement is cor-
rect, mark the spot you want to cut with one mark
from a sharp pencil, then cut off half that line.

He was a firm believer in doing a job with ded-
ication and determination, and doing it right the
first time. And it didn't matter whether it was a job
large or small, when it was completed, the work

(back) Joe, Merv, Phil, (front) Mary, Atlee, Ellen
Early 2000s

area was to be clean. Not only clean, but cleaner than it was when the task began.

When giving instruction that was met with, "Well, I'll try," his response was, "You have to do more than try!" That statement was frustrating to children, but the logic became much clearer as time passed.

Each of the boys started working with Atlee, then Merv moved to customer service, Joe drove truck, and Phil worked in maintenance.

Noah Troyer was the owner of Holmes Lumber, and Atlee always enjoyed working for him. The workday began with Atlee sitting inside the wide windows of Noah's office, having a few minutes' chat before heading out. Whether a job went exceptionally well or mistakes were made, Noah always treated Atlee with respect.

By the mid-1980s, Atlee was experiencing back pain and could no longer do the strenuous carpentry work that had occupied him for so long. He bought a 15-passenger van and started his taxi service among the Amish community, a job he came to love. His travels took him throughout the United States, and he traveled to every state of the Union except Hawaii. He made seven trips to the West and was in Alaska once. When the situation permitted,

Mary accompanied Atlee on these trips, an opportunity they both greatly enjoyed.

Even more than travel and seeing the sights, Atlee enjoyed the friendships that developed and the conversations engaged in on these trips.

"It doesn't matter if I've never seen you before, once you're in my van, you're no longer a stranger!" was Atlee's statement and philosophy. He especially enjoyed being able to share what God had done in his life, and the conversations he recalled best were those centered around the Lord Jesus Christ.

This job also provided its moments of humor. There was the time Atlee had taken a vanload of Amish to Indiana, including a man named Danny.

Atlee and Mary in Arizona

On the way home, they needed to make a pit stop and buy a few snacks. Atlee's passengers went in to do their shopping, while Atlee stayed in the van.

It had been a long day, and he just wanted to get home. He could see his passengers through the windows of the store, and having the tendency to talk to himself, he good-naturedly urged them on. "C'mon, people, hurry up! Let's go home!" They finally completed their purchases, straggled out to the van, and all went home happy.

A week later, Atlee received a call to take Danny's son-in-law somewhere. During the drive, the son-in-law asked Atlee if he had taken folks to Indiana, and if they had wanted to stop on the way

Atlee and Mary on their trip to Alaska

home. He then told Atlee that on the previous trip to Indiana, Danny hadn't exited the van at that last stop but had remained in the back seat. Through a splendid effort of self-control, he had contained his laughter as Atlee admonished those that were in the store.

Three weeks after having the son-in-law tell him that story, Atlee was asked to taxi Danny. As Danny approached the van, Atlee told him to sit up front and when he (Atlee) talked, then Danny was supposed to answer! Danny got a big laugh out of that, as did Atlee. Danny also confirmed that Atlee had said nothing unkind.

Once, while taxiing Amish, Atlee stopped with his passengers at a restaurant. They were in a hurry, so Atlee, ordering first, asked for a bowl of fruit. He thought that would be a quick order to fill. All the others decided this was a great idea, so they also ordered fruit bowls, which caused the restaurant to run out of fruit. The restaurant manager then had to send someone to the grocery store to get more, which of course ended up taking a long time.

These trips were full of good times, camaraderie, and even a few adventures. There were times when fuel ran low, winding mountain roads caused great concern to those sitting on the drop-off side, and treacherous driving conditions were encountered. There were even a few accidents, which fortunately never resulted in any serious injuries.

Atlee became known in the Amish community as an excellent driver, and he continued his taxi work for almost twenty-five years.

In 2006, Atlee was on the road taxiing Amish every day except one (not counting Sundays).

Atlee was taxiing some of his friends on the day he turned eighty years old. They hadn't known it was his birthday, but he informed them of the fact. Then, every once in a while, he would gleefully say, "Oh yeah, I'm eighty today!" and would push the gas pedal even harder.

Unfortunately, not all of Atlee's experiences on the road were quite so pleasant.

April 8, 2010. Atlee was headed north on Interstate 77 in his 15-passenger van. At the time, he had a side business of selling windows and was going to Akron to pick up an order for a customer.

Needing to make a pit stop, he took the exit ramp at Arlington Road and pulled into a gas station. He slowed down, rounded the corner into the parking lot, and pulled up towards a parking space.

Suddenly, before the van even came to a stop, the passenger door flew open, and a woman jumped into the seat. Atlee usually locked the doors, but it had slipped his mind this time.

It was immediately obvious to Atlee that this woman was not in a normal state of mind; she was fidgeting and mumbling about being cold and wet. Suddenly she said, "Give me your money!"

Still trying to grasp what exactly was going on, Atlee refused. Without warning, the woman jumped out of her seat at him and began beating him with her fists. She tried to grab his wallet, and Atlee suddenly found himself quite busy getting the van into park, trying to hang on to his wallet, and fending off her flying fists. At one point she threatened to cut his throat, and afterward, he discovered a spot on his neck that was scratched and bleeding, but he did not actually see a weapon at any point. Somehow, during the melee, he managed to turn off the engine, remove the keys from the ignition, and stick them in his pocket.

The driver's door opened (Atlee didn't remember if he or the woman opened it), and he exited the van, with the stranger immediately after him, pummeling away. Between blows, she was still trying to get his wallet, and broke the chain that attached it to his belt. So there they were, a woman beating up an eighty-year-old man in a busy parking lot, and nobody stopped to help. At one point, Atlee tried to reach in through the open door to blow the horn, but she dragged him away. He pushed down the lock as she pulled him away from the van, and tried, again, to push her away, but she had a firm grip on his shirtsleeve with one hand as she pounded away with the other.

Realizing that he was losing strength, he managed one more hard push. As she staggered back, he pulled away from her and jumped into the van, slamming the door. Not a second too soon; she leaped forward, and the door had scarcely latched before she grabbed the handle and pulled. If he had not locked the door earlier, he would not have had time to do so before she would have yanked it open again. She then ran around to the passenger side and tried to get in, but all the doors were locked.

Quickly starting the van, Atlee drove away. He was scratched and bruised and had lost his glasses, but kept his wallet.

It all happened so fast that he scarcely had time to be afraid during the attack, but what he had to think about later was how close he came to not getting the door closed as he jumped back in the van, and what could have happened had he not locked it earlier. By the grace of God, he suffered only minor injuries.

EIGHTEEN

Robbie Weaver grew up on a small farm about one mile west of where Atlee and Mary were raising their young family. As a boy, Robbie would occasionally be sent to their place to make a phone call: perhaps to order feed, summon the vet for an ailing animal, or for other various reasons.

As this usually occurred during the day when Atlee was at work, it was Mary who would answer the knock on the door. Robbie remembers her smile and her kindness; he never had to make the call himself, as she would always do it for him.

Time passed, and Robbie got married. He and his wife, Sara Ann, had four children: Mary Ellen, Steven, Wilma, and Joey.

In 1994, Atlee took Robbie and his family to Canada on a fishing trip. It was a weeklong trip, and by the time it was over, Atlee and Robbie had formed a deep friendship. It didn't take the family long to discover that Atlee had a living relationship with Jesus Christ. He freely shared his love of God, and Robbie and his family found Atlee's love of life, sense of humor, and optimistic outlook to be an inspiration to them.

Atlee did his best to make the trip enjoyable for the entire family, and the children began to call him "Canada Daudy." (On a later trip to the Smoky Mountains, he was known as "Smoky Daudy.")

Morning came to the lakeside cabin. The jagged line of pine trees emerged from the dawn, and mist swirled gently across the mirrored surface of the lake. Gray clouds hung low in the sky, and the scent of rain was in the air.

With breakfast over, Atlee and Robbie walked outside. There was only an occasional sprinkle of rain, and Atlee said, "Rob, it's not raining too hard. Don't you think we should go fishing?" Robbie agreed, so they, along with Steven, got into the boat and headed out onto the lake.

As they started out, Robbie casually remarked, "Hm, I hope we have enough gas."

They traveled about a mile and a half to their chosen spot, baited their hooks, and began fishing. Nobody said too much as they relaxed, caught a few fish, and enjoyed the quiet of the wilderness morning. The rain gradually increased, and Atlee suggested heading back to the cabin. Robbie reeled in his hook.

"Okay, if I have enough gas."

Atlee's face grew serious.

"Rob, you know better! We're going to have enough, right?"

"Well, I hope so!"

Robbie chuckled to himself. He had checked the gas before they had left the dock, and knew there was more than enough to get them back to the cabin.

Atlee was silent for a moment, then said, "There are two paddles here, and you know who's going to row if we run out of gas; it's not going to be me!"

Robbie just laughed, and they started the long run back to the dock.

After a few minutes of skimming across the rain-dappled lake, Robbie casually positioned himself so that Atlee's view of the motor was blocked. Glancing at Atlee to make sure he wasn't watching, Robbie reached back and pushed the kill switch, then quickly released it. The engine sputtered, then resumed its steady hum.

Atlee's head spun around.

"Rob!" He shook his finger and said, "You remember what I said; I'm not going to paddle!"

Every few minutes, the scenario was repeated: the motor sputtered, Atlee reminded Robbie of his aversion to paddling, and Robbie laughed to himself.

Finally, still a considerable distance from shore, Robbie opened wide the throttle and held it open; no hesitations, no sputters. As they approached the dock, it dawned on Atlee what Robbie had been doing. Shaking his head and giving a final wag of his finger, he said, "Rob, Rob, you're nothing but a Weaver!"

It was after lunch a few days later, and most of the adults were not in the mood to go fishing. Mary Ellen and Steven wanted to go, so Atlee volunteered to take them out on the boat. After a while,

Robbie went on a walk, taking a pair of binoculars with him. He found himself on a hillside overlooking the lake, and spotted the boat in the distance. Curious as to how the fishing was going, he raised the binoculars and focused on the goings-on in the boat.

Atlee was in the middle of baiting a hook for Steven; Mary Ellen already had her line in the water. With the bait securely on the hook, Steven raised the rod up and back, preparing to cast. As the hook danced precariously over the occupants of the boat, Robbie saw Atlee duck low, eyes following the bait as it dangled over his head.

A heave of a little arm, a splash as hook and worm entered the water, and Atlee rose up from his crouch. By that time, a fish too clever to be caught had devoured another worm, and another round of baiting and ducking began.

And so went the next hour. Atlee assisted the children in their endeavors, baiting the hooks and, occasionally, removing a fish. And every time a line was cast, Atlee would lower himself as far as possible to avoid the barbed steel that was whipping by overhead.

Atlee never did have the time to fish for himself that day, but his was the biggest smile of all when they returned to the dock.

A few years later, Atlee and Robbie's family were on another fishing trip, along with a few other couples. This time they were in the northern reaches of Canada. After traveling a long way, they came to a gas station with a sign that said, "Next Gas Station, 90 Miles."

Robbie said, "Atlee, don't you think we should get gas here?"

Atlee didn't seem to be worried.

"Oh, I think we can go on."

Robbie and his friend Ray, one of the other men along on the trip, were concerned. The van was heavily loaded, and they were towing a large boat. Fuel consumption had to be quite high.

Another sixty miles spun by beneath the wheels, and suddenly they all heard a *beep beep.*

"What is that, Atlee?"

Atlee didn't seem too perturbed.

"Oh, that's what happens just before we run out of gas."

Robbie and Ray glanced at each other. Their unease rose as mile after mile of tundra rolled by. Raindrops splashed off the roadway and soaked the countryside. The beeper kept sounding its alert, but Atlee didn't appear to hear it. Ray tapped Robbie on the shoulder.

"Rob, what can we do?"

Robbie cleared his throat.

"Atlee, we do have an empty gas can in the boat, but if we run out, you will be the guy that's gonna walk to get gas; I will not!"

There was no response from Atlee.

A few more miles passed in silence, then, far ahead, they saw a tractor-trailer. It was heading the same direction as they were, and they slowly caught up with it.

Ray spoke up from the back seat.

"Atlee, I read somewhere that if you drive really close behind a big truck, they will break the wind for you, and you can just kind of coast along. You don't use nearly as much gas."

"Oh really? Thank you!" Atlee pushed harder on the accelerator and narrowed the gap between van and semi. Then, swinging smoothly into the left lane, he passed the truck. Again, the beeper sounded loud in the quiet of the van. The tension mounted. Atlee had always been a trustworthy driver, but this did seem to be a bit reckless.

Finally, there was the sight of a small building in the distance. Could it be...? And sure enough, there was the sign. Gas! Sighs of relief could be heard, and conversation started up again. Atlee pulled up to the pump, and everyone got out to stretch. Robbie walked around to where Atlee was pumping the gas.

"Well, Atlee, that was a bit close, wasn't it?"

Atlee smiled.

"Oh, not really. I have a reserve tank on this van. We could have gone another forty miles at least!"

So Atlee had the last laugh this time, but whether in joking with each other or in serious discussions, Atlee and Robbie's friendship remained strong.

On another trip to Canada, they were staying in a log cabin beside a river. Off the bank on the opposite side of the river was a swimming area with a twenty-five to thirty-foot diving board. Atlee and Robbie's family found it interesting to watch people diving off the board. Some did it apparently without fear, some took a bit of coaxing, and others backed out and returned down the ladder.

After watching for awhile, Atlee said, "You know what? That looks interesting! If any of you will jump off that board, I'll be right behind you!"

There was much talk and a lot of daring, but nobody took Atlee up on the challenge.

Robbie was ordained as deacon in the Amish church in 1997. Shortly after, Atlee talked to him and encouraged him. He said, "Okay, Rob, when you're preaching the Word, I don't want you to be looking in the corners or at the ceiling. Don't be checking out the spider webs. Face the people."

This bit of advice from a seasoned pastor is something that Robbie has not forgotten.

One snowy winter day, Atlee picked up Robbie's family and a few others to take them somewhere. Everyone was in high spirits, and the hubbub of conversation filled the van.

Suddenly, above the chatter, Atlee asked, "Hey, would you all like some donuts?"

Hearty approval was given to this suggestion, and in a few blocks, Atlee turned into a parking lot. A large, empty parking lot, where he then proceeded to perform "donuts" in the snow with his 15-passenger van.

Needless to say, these were not the donuts his

passengers were expecting, and while Atlee enjoyed the fun, most of his passengers were less than enthusiastic.

Atlee didn't let a little snow keep him off the road

NINETEEN

August 19, 2007. It was a warm summer morning. Atlee, Mary, and two of their sons, Joe and Phil, were headed for southern Ohio. There was a Barkman family reunion planned at a farm owned by Atlee's brother Raymond, and most of the family planned on being there. It was a pleasant drive through the hilly countryside, and they arrived before the rest of the family. As noontime approached, more of the Barkmans showed up, and soon the air filled with the noise of conversation and children playing. Atlee's brothers—Bert, Emanuel, and Raymond—were all there, and talk became animated as nephews, nieces, and cousins joined in.

It was a fascinating scene, seeing the four patriarchs of the Barkman families together. They were customarily viewed as fathers and uncles, but to see them interacting as brothers added a new dimension to their characters and personalities. These men raised the bar for those following after by the lives they lived and the examples they set.

The outing took place in a field bordered by a stream, with towering trees lining the three-to-four-foot banks. The water, shallow at this time of the year, gurgled and swirled over the large flat rocks that lined the creek bed. Raymond's sons, being an adventuresome crew, had at some point in

Atlee and his brothers
(left to right) Raymond, Atlee, Emanuel & Albert

time built a twenty-foot platform on the north bank of the creek and attached a rope high in one of the trees. By climbing onto the platform, stepping into the loop at the end of the rope, and leaping into thin air, they could experience an exhilarating ride.

As time passed, the conversation turned to the rope swing, and one nephew, in fun, challenged the elderly men to take a ride.

"Well, I'll do it if Atlee will," joked Emanuel, and immediately Atlee was on his feet and heading for the creek. Laughter and cheers arose as he crossed the creek towards the platform on the opposite bank. The laughter abated, however, as he climbed the bank at the base of the platform. He wasn't actually going to do it, was he?

As Atlee ascended the ladder, his family realized he wasn't bluffing, and that's when the prayers began.

"Don't do it!" exclaimed a niece, while Mary turned her face away; she couldn't bear to watch. There were murmurs of dismay, and the laughter changed to shouts of instruction.

"Put your foot in that loop!"

"Take ahold above the knot!"

Atlee inched his way forward on the platform, sat down on the edge, and gripped the sixty-foot rope firmly. He slipped his foot into the loop at the end, gave a few tugs, and then off he went. Some members of the family shouted with enthusiasm, while others exclaimed in fear as he swooped down across the creek, just a few feet above the rocks. Up he sailed among the trees on the opposite bank, and then back, each seventy-five-foot arc seeming to last forever.

As he swung back and forth, his momentum decreasing, two of his nephews positioned themselves on the bank and on his tenth pass, caught him and brought him to a stop. The family released a collective sigh of relief as he let go of the rope and rolled onto the creek bank. The rest of the afternoon passed by pleasantly enough, but the details of it are now mostly forgotten, overshadowed by the visual of that 77-year-old man swinging on the rope like a giant pendulum.

On the way home, Atlee said that from the moment it was mentioned, he knew he was going to do it. It makes sense; this is the guy that rode motorcycles and raced horses in his youth.

Quite some time passed before Atlee told the family that when he stepped off the platform, the rope slipped, and only the toe of his boot was in the loop.

In 2013, Atlee's eyesight worsened, and in 2014, he gave up driving altogether. With Mary no longer able to drive, they depended on their children and others to take them where they needed to go. Atlee, however, refused to be discouraged by obstacles such as poor eyesight.

"I'm going to get new eyes someday anyway," he said, and smiled.

After living across the road from Mary's parents for thirty-nine years, they had sold the house in 1990 and built a new one approximately one mile southeast of Benton, where they lived for

Getting the mail

the next twenty-five years. Then, in 2015, they moved to The Commons at Walnut Hills.

Atlee and Mary spent their days in their apartment at the Commons, where they frequently entertained visitors. Family members, friends, and former neighbors stopped by to chat and to check on their welfare. Atlee's enthusiasm for life and Mary's steady, quiet friendship and her heart for "the least of these" were an inspiration to many.

They enjoyed having someone take them for a drive or out to lunch where they often encountered old friends and acquaintances. Atlee couldn't see very well and found it difficult to recognize faces, even from a short distance, so he was always pleased when friends made themselves known. Many are familiar with the phrase he so frequently used in greeting: "Lobe der Herr!" (Praise the Lord!)

Waiting for a parade, 2016   Lunchtime, 2017

Sunday, November 29, 2015. Atlee and Mary were in church, and the congregation started the second verse of the closing hymn. Atlee felt a sadness steal over him. Tears welled up in his eyes and trickled down his cheeks. He didn't know why; it had been an inspiring sermon.

Throughout the afternoon, it felt as though a cloud had descended on him. He couldn't pinpoint its source, but it enveloped him like a blanket, smothering all thoughts of hope and cheer. He called his son Joe and asked him to come over. When Joe walked in the front door, Atlee broke down in tears and was barely able to speak.

The next six months were a struggle for Atlee and Mary. During this time period, Atlee suffered a hiatal hernia, a fall, and various medical issues. It is possible that his pancreatic and liver cancer, undetected by doctors, was already having a negative effect on his body.

Atlee was very emotional, and wept at the slightest cause. For a period of time, their children took turns staying overnight with Atlee and Mary.

It was difficult for Atlee to understand why this was happening to him. He did not consider himself susceptible to stress, and perhaps that was part of the problem. Much had happened in the last year: the move to the Commons, the degradation of his eyesight, and the end of his twenty-five-year taxiing career.

Many times he would say, "Atlee Barkman, what is **wrong** with you?" He struggled to understand, but yet, in what was a tremendous inspiration to family and friends, his trust in God did not waver. He would say, "Well, I'm being tested, and I'll come out brighter on the other side."

It was truly a walk of faith for him. He had never encountered something like this before, and he didn't know why it happened or when it was going to end. He just kept on, spiritually speaking, putting one foot in front of the other and trusting God for each step.

This episode was also a challenge for the family. They had never seen Atlee go through such a valley, even during the many other challenges in his life. They could only walk alongside as best as possible, encouraging him and praying.

As time passed, so, finally, did the depression. Although Atlee's body continued to weaken, his spirits improved and he regained his joyful, happy self. And when it was over, he didn't waste any time bemoaning the fact or asking questions with no answers. One of the strengths of his character was the ability to leave the past behind and move on.

May 2016. Atlee and Mary were sitting in Boyd and Wurthmann Restaurant in Berlin with one of their sons, waiting for their lunch. Talk turned to the rope swing ride; a family member at the reunion had taken a video of it, but Atlee and Mary couldn't find their copy of the DVD. Atlee's brother Bert said he would send his copy from Florida, and Atlee could hardly wait to see it.

"We should go down there, and I could take that ride again," said Atlee with a slight smile, knowing the reaction he would get.

"No!" Mary shook her head firmly, and their son laughed, but couldn't refrain from saying, "I think we'd have to stop you this time!"

Atlee wasn't as strong physically as he had been nine years ago: diabetes, depression, and macular degeneration had all taken a toll. A visit to the ER with chest pains, a fall that skinned his nose, and a less-than-certain stride were some of the markers that age had left on his body.

And yet his family and friends could attest that when asked, "How are you?" or "How was your day?" the answer was almost always positive.

"I've had a good day!" was usually followed by

a more detailed explanation. The love of God, the mystery of His grace and mercy, and the blessings to be found in Scripture were frequently the topic of discussion and the reason why Atlee considered most of his days to be very good.

Atlee and Mary treasured their family, and greatly enjoyed the first Sunday evening of every month, when children, grandchildren, and great-grandchildren would all pile into the house. At this writing, there are seven grandchildren and eight great-grandchildren.

Atlee and Mary were the first to remind others that they were not perfect and that reaching the so-called golden years did not make the race any easier to run. They encountered the same spiritual battles and emotional issues that everyone faces, and added to that were the challenges of a body that just did not want to respond as it used to.

At eighty-six years old, Atlee stated that he couldn't say life was unfair. As he looked back, he saw God moving in his life and protecting him, long before he ever cared about God at all.

He told his family of how he would sit and meditate on the grace that saved him, and of the events leading to the crucifixion of Christ. He would close his eyes and imagine that night in the garden and then the journey to the judgment halls of Pilate and Herod. He could see the torture that Christ took for us, and then he imagined the procession winding up the hill of Calvary. He saw Christ being placed on the cross and found himself flinching as, in his mind's eye, he watched the hammer descend upon the spike that would hold Christ on that instrument of death.

Sunday forenoon, 10:00 am. Atlee settles into his chair and tucks the cushion in beside him. The pain in his side has been nagging him. It's not too bad today, but he didn't feel well enough to go to church. Mary is reading in her chair beside him. He reclines and closes his eyes, but can't sleep. His eyes are dim with age, but the images of memory are still sharp as the years of his life spin by.

The minutes slip by, and Atlee dozes. He wakes as Mary turns a page, and a smile crosses his face. As he drifts off to sleep again, he quietly breathes an old, familiar phrase, "Lobe der Herr..."

On the morning of September 28, 2007, Mom, Dad, Ellen, and I (Phil) went on a weekend trip to Kalona, Iowa. We were going to visit Uncle Eli (Mom's brother) and Aunt Katie and any of the other relatives who would drop in.

We had planned to leave at 8:00 am, but when I arrived at Mom and Dad's house around 7:55, Mom

was doing paperwork. I don't know why she chose to do it then, but she was in her chair, figuring and writing away. Dad, of course, was ready to go. This was the man who was seldom late and didn't like it when he was.

Now, if Mom had been just a few minutes late, there wouldn't have been a big problem, but as she continued her work, Dad became increasingly impatient. He was a Barkman, ready to go **now**, and she was a Swartzentruber; time is meant to be utilized efficiently. So Dad kept pushing her and she pushed back, saying he was only slowing her down. She finally finished at a bit past 8:30, and we were underway by 8:45.

No harm done, but it was interesting to watch these two personalities, so blended and accommodating over the years, yet still so different within the circle of their life and love.

Sunday evening at Eli and Katie's home. We were sitting in the living room, talking: Dad and Mom, Eli and Katie, Jim and Sherrie, Joe and Deb, Ellen, and myself.

Dad was the center of attention; he was telling stories of the old days and how he got to know Mom. For Dad, these were great stories to tell; for Mom, they drew far too much attention to herself. There was nothing wrong with the stories, as they were not embarrassing or out of place, but Mom became uncomfortable. She leaned over, placed her hand on Dad's arm, and told him to stop. He wanted to know why; these are great stories! She quietly but firmly told him that if he continued, she would walk out. She leaned closer to make her point, and Dad said, "Well, if you come any closer, I'll give you a kiss!"

This, of course, was a great crowd-pleaser, since we were already enjoying the scene immensely. Mom then did something entirely unexpected; she reached up and lightly slapped Dad's face. We were almost rolling on the floor at this point. Dad feigned great protest, and then proceeded to tell the story anyway. It was the account of how she would stand in the small space between the stove and the cupboard when he would arrive to visit her brothers. Mom didn't walk out as Dad continued the story, of course; the anticipation of Dad recounting the story was worse than the actual telling.

I am fascinated by something I saw in Dad. When he was in a group of talkers and the conversation was too fast for him to follow or concerning subjects he didn't know or care for, he was content to sit back and listen. He wasn't one to talk just to be heard. But when it was a subject about which he was passionate, or when people drew him out, he became quite animated and had no problem expressing himself.

Dad could be ever so serious and passionate at the same time, talking about the love of God. He could also be the life of the party, especially when surrounded by family, brothers, nephews, and family in general. They had high respect for him and enjoyed "getting him going." He loved talking about the past. With his ever-ready wit and humor, his stories of exploits and adventures were all well received.

He was always well liked by youth, both in his family and the church. I think this was because he was never a dried-up, dull "old person."

On Friday evening, the 26th of May, 2017, Dad went to bed feeling fine. He woke up around 2:00 am and wanted to roll over, but couldn't because of a sharp pain just below his ribcage on his right side. After seeing his doctor, he was scheduled for a CAT scan and X-ray on June 6, and on the 16th, discovered there was a tumor on his liver. From there he went to see a specialist on June 26, and on July 5 the doctor performed a biopsy.

On July 13 he received the diagnosis of both liver and pancreatic cancer. He was very weak and in quite a bit of pain, so he was prescribed a painkiller. In spite of all this, he very much wanted to attend a wedding on the 22nd, and did so. The exertion of the day weakened him even more, and on the 24th, we signed up with hospice, at his request. Hospice provided excellent care, but from that point on he went into a steady decline.

On August 3, 2017, at 10:03 am, with Mom and Ellen at his side, Dad took a few long, last breaths and slipped away.

For Mom and Dad, knowing God was not merely an exercise in religion, but an intimate friendship with and worship of their heavenly Father. Their faith in the living Christ carried them through all that life threw their way. Listening to the voice of the Spirit and experiencing the comfort He brings made the struggle worthwhile and brought them joy in their latter years.

ONE OF DAD'S
FAVORITE SCRIPTURES

Blessed be the God and Father

of our Lord Jesus Christ,

which according to his abundant

mercy hath begotten us again unto

a lively hope by the resurrection of

Jesus Christ from the dead,

To an inheritance incorruptible,

and undefiled, and that fadeth not away,

reserved in heaven for you,

Who are kept by the power of God

through faith unto salvation ready

to be revealed in the last time.

EXCERPTS FROM 2011 SERMON

A lot of you people probably don't know me, and that makes no difference. I don't know a lot of you, and it makes no difference. But as long as we know the man, the man Christ Jesus, that hung on the middle cross. That song... very touching, the man that hung on the middle cross and died all alone. People, think about that tonight. That is the Lord Jesus that hung on the middle cross. And He died all alone, all alone... do we believe that tonight? That Christ Jesus died all alone.

I greet you in that name. That is a name that we want to use, we want to use it very carefully. When I was a young man, I was a sinner and I used that name in vain. But you know what makes me so excited? I get so blessed and I get an inspiration from the Word of God and meditating upon the Lord

Jesus Christ, and on the Trinity, that God Almighty forgave me for using His name and the name of His Son in vain. Do you think that I'm excited about salvation through Jesus Christ? When He hung on the middle cross and God turned away from Him so he could die for this man that was so lost in sin and didn't care about God at all.

How do you feel tonight about God? How do you feel tonight about the Lord Jesus Christ? How do you feel about the Holy Ghost tonight? How is it with us tonight?

We sang that song, that if the whole world were mine, if the whole world were yours, it would be a gift far too small to give to the Lord Jesus Christ. But you know what He wants? He wants our heart. He wants our life. He wants all that we've got. I think of the Psalms where he says, "Bless the Lord, oh my soul, and all that is within me, bless his Holy name!"

We are members of the body of Jesus Christ. The Bible says in Romans 7:4 "We are married to Him that rose from the dead." You know what that is like? Is that your experience? Is that my experience tonight, that we're married to Him that rose from the dead? And you can't get any closer than to be married. It's like us, like a body... like your body and my body tonight. We've got a head, and we function according to the head. Why did I walk up here? Was it because my feet wanted to go first? No, it was in the head. The head told me to go up those steps.

That's the way it is with the church of Jesus Christ. We fit in there. We are born into the body of Jesus Christ. We are a member of the body of Jesus Christ. Jesus Christ is as precious as anything can ever get or anybody can ever get. The church will move according to the Lord Jesus Christ.

Tonight, if I have a title, it is, "The Kingdom of God is Within Man." The Kingdom of God is in every saint, and in that kingdom there is a King, and that King is the Lord Jesus Christ, and He rules in that kingdom. He has power and He has authority, and the church moves according to the head. And that's the Lord Jesus Christ. And I'm glad tonight that I know that.

You read that in Luke 17:21; "The kingdom of God is within you." And I'm looking at you people and you're looking at me. Now, is it true tonight that the kingdom of God dwells within me? Is it true that the kingdom of God dwells in you and you have a king that rules in your life, one that has power and authority to lead us all the way to Glory? And the church today is enjoying itself in Jesus Christ. The church is united because we follow the head, the

Lord Jesus Christ. And the Bible says, "The kingdom comes not by word only, but it comes by power." So tonight, if you and I are Christians, then we have power within us to resist temptations.

Satan is not going to leave us alone till we go the last time. Then he's done tempting us. But we don't have to yield to him. We don't have to yield to the temptations or the things of the world. God is a God of love.

The Bible, in Isaiah 57:15, talks about the lofty one, the Holy One, which is the same Person that inhabits eternity. God is everywhere present. You can't hide. It makes no difference where we go, you can go out in the woods in the dark of the night, way back in, but you cannot hide from God, because it says, "He inhabiteth eternity." He's everywhere present. But what is so amazing and what is so wonderful, He says, "I dwell... with him also that is of a contrite and humble spirit, to revive the spirit of the humble, and to revive the heart of the contrite ones." He wants us to have revival as we grow older, and the young people to have revival as well.

And think about it tonight, friends; let's realize that Jesus Christ was here, and He went back to heaven, but He didn't leave us alone. He sent the Holy Spirit to come to teach us and to lead us, at least partly in truth? No, it says, "To lead us in all truth." The Holy Spirit will teach us and lead us in all truth, so that the gates of Hell cannot prevail against the body, against the church of Jesus Christ. Now you can join all the congregations you want to join, you can join one, you can join two or six. That does not make you a Christian. Men and women, young men, old men, darkening the doors... the door frames of a church house will not make them a Christian. Believe that.

But when we go to church, what do we do? The best foot comes forward. But what about when we're outside the church house? What do the people think of us when they see us out on the street? What we need to be are born again people, born by the Spirit of God and a part of the body of Jesus Christ. I don't know where I fit in in that body, I really don't, but I want to be faithful because of the love of God. Think of the love of God. "For God so loved the world." Can you imagine that tonight? Knowing what Jesus Christ was going to go through, and God so loved the world. I think there's a lot of weight on that word, "so." God so loved the world that He gave the best He had; it was like Himself coming. Can we grasp tonight, that God sent His son down to this earth to be an example to us, to preach the gospel of Jesus Christ by parables, by His way of life, and then took him back to Heaven? Now what did He do? Now what is going on? Now who is here? Do we believe tonight that you and I are here in Christ's stead? Do you believe that?

The Bible says, "For by thy words thou shall be justified and by thy words thou shall be condemned" (Matthew 12:37). Now, God put us here in Christ's stead. You go back into 2 Corinthians 5:17, there it says, "Therefore if any man be in Christ, he is..." What? "...he is a new creature." He is a new creature. You probably, as well as I, know people that said they made a decision for God, and they lived the same way they did before. There was no change. "Therefore any man be in Christ, he is a new creature; old things are passed away; behold, all things are become new." I haven't reached that yet... I really haven't. I still have those temptations, I still lack in words, I still lack in actions. I would like to be perfect. The Bible says... I could quote it in German but maybe not in English... but it talks about being perfect.

When I think of what we sang tonight, "The man on the middle cross." Just think of it, that we are here in His stead. And if you'd go on in 2 Corinthians 5:18, it says there that "God... hath given to us the ministry of reconciliation." Now, that's not just for the preacher. That's for every born-again individual; every one that accepts the Lord Jesus Christ has received that privilege. You know, I call it a privilege and a responsibility to hold forth the word of God. And it goes on to say that He has not imputed our trespasses against us, but he has given us the word of reconciliation. Are we hungry for the Word of God?

We all have sinned and come short of the glory of God. But in God's goodness we can say tonight we have peace with God and our fellow man. It's really important to have peace with God. Because one thing the Bible says, "But grow in grace, and in knowledge of our Lord and Saviour Jesus Christ" (2 Peter 3:18). That is growing in favor with God. Now how are we going to grow in favor with God? We need to read the Word of God. We need to be hungry for the Word of God. We must love to read the Word of God, and then proclaim it in the way we live it. The believer will live his life. If we say we believe in the Lord Jesus Christ, we'll live that way. I'm not saying that we're not going to be tempted or that we're not going to fall by the wayside. I'm not saying that we're not going to make mistakes or that we're going be always kind to our companion.

We might not always be kind to our children, or the children to the parents. We make mistakes, but in this kingdom, with that king, which is the Lord Jesus Christ, there is power and authority and there's everything that we need to live an overcoming life, starting in the home. Starting in the home, loving our companion, being kind to our companion, we husbands to our wives, wives to your husbands, that's in the kingdom.

Children, obey your parents in the Lord. Don't be rude to your parents. I always told my children, "You cannot argue, you dare not argue with Mom. You can discuss issues with Mom, but you dare not walk away and be angry at Mom. You dare not do that. She brought you into the world and went through pain and agony to bring into the world and take care of you." So there's everything in the kingdom that we need to live right in the world. Then we can go to town and we live right. We show to the people that there's a way to heaven, and that's by the way of the cross. We die to self; we give ourselves to the Lord Jesus Christ. Give him all we've got.

Going to 2 Corinthians 5:20; we're here in Christ's stead. Be reconciled to God, because it says, in verse 21, "For He hath made Him to be sin for us, who knew no sin; that we might be made the righteousness of God in Him." (Hits pulpit) People, we can be made the righteousness of God on the earth, if we do the will of God! Can you imagine? Do I imagine and do I believe that tonight, we can be made the righteousness of God in Jesus Christ? Because He died all alone. Can you imagine that? That's touching... that someone would die for me, all alone. God himself turned away from Him, so that He could die for me. So that I could live right, and enjoy my life. I'm looking at you; are you enjoying your life in Christ? Are you enjoying yourself among yourselves like a family?

Young people, remember, if you're a Christian, you're born into the body of Jesus Christ. The power... the kingdom came not only by word, it came also by power. We have power to overcome sin. Oh, look at it, we can have victory over Satan, over the devil. I say, the Bible says, that we are sealed the Holy Spirit of promise. And if we don't break that seal, I don't care how many fiery darts that old Satan throws at us, they'll glance off. But start flirting with the world, start flirting with sin, those darts will come in and they'll make you miserable. Oh, they'll make us miserable if we do that. But who wants to be miserable?

And serving the Lord; let's do it and rejoice in the Lord Jesus Christ. And we don't have to go around shouting about it, we can have this personal relationship, like I said, growing in grace and in knowledge of our Lord and Saviour Jesus Christ and have good communion. It's amazing when I talk about it, it's amazing when I think about it, that we little creatures of the dust can have relationship communion with God. God is real! Sometimes when I pray, it sometimes seems to me like I could almost reach Him, you know, almost touch Him, but He's in heaven. But He's here on the earth through the Spirit. So we commune with Him, then we read the Word, have good relationship that way, and then we obey the Word. And you know what? If we do that, we'll bring forth fruit. And if you and I want to be filled with the love of God and the joy of the Lord, we must be workers in the kingdom. We dare not be idle.

Why are people out there that will bow to stone? They'll bow to wood; they'll worship the sun. Someone has left down, somebody quit teaching the gospel, the full gospel. We need the full gospel to persuade people that there is a God in heaven, and there is the Lord Jesus Christ, and that the Holy Spirit is here. He came to bring comfort to us, to teach us, and to lead us into all truth.

The Bible says in the Lord's prayer, "Thy will be done in earth, as it is in heaven" (Matthew 6:10). How hard are we working to make it here on the earth as it is in Heaven? Now if we have a conversation afterwards, we all say heaven is a pure place. Heaven is holy, and it'll stay that way. Are we trying to make it that way here on earth? Thy will be done on earth, as it is in Heaven. "And lead us not into temptation... for Thine is the kingdom, and the power, and the glory, for ever." Lead us not into temptation? He never will. Never will! God stands at the door and knocks, and here it is; when we read the Word of God, it'll cleanse us.

I remember back in Cincinnati; we lived there in the early '50's and I got hungry for the Word of God. I'd sooner read it than eat; ask my wife. And I read the Word of God and I was hungry for it and I came to that scripture, Hebrews 4:12, where it says, "For the Word of God is quick, and powerful, and sharper than any two-edged sword, piercing even to the dividing asunder of soul and spirit..." It is so powerful that it will cleanse us. It's so sharp. That verse talks about the joints and marrow and of the discerning of the thoughts and intents of the heart. I'm a simple man, and I believe that. If I believe the

Word of God, then God Almighty will take sin out of me, He'll cut sin out of me, but He will not mar my flesh, my bone, my bone marrow, or anything. But it's so powerful—the Word of God and the work of God—that He'll cut sin out and not mar the body. Amazing, friends! It's amazing that the Word of God is that powerful, and will make saints out of us! We are here in Christ's stead. Yeah, I know the preacher's supposed to! No, it's everyone, everyone that accepts the Lord Jesus Christ has received that gift to talk about the Lord Jesus Christ. What's so hard about talking to people about the Lord Jesus Christ? As we go through life, let's remember that He is the God of the universe and we're here in Christ's stead.

John 14:15 says, "If ye love me, keep my commandments." And the commandments are not hard. They're not grievous. They can be kept, but not on our own strength. We have the spirit of God And Jesus then said, in verse 23, "...we will come unto him, and make our abode with him." He is gonna come and He and the Father are going to live in us. Now isn't that amazing? That the God of heaven, the God of the universe, the God that put the stars out there with the tips of His fingers—and He gave them all names—would want to live within us? That's touching. I read those scriptures, that God wants to live within me. And I can say tonight, I think He lives within me, and I'm not boastful, because the Bible says in Galatians 6:14, "But God forbid that I should glory..." I'm going say this here. Don't glory in your beauty. Don't glory in your strengths. Don't glory in your education. Don't glory in your background. Because that verse says, don't glory, "... save in the cross of our Lord Jesus Christ." Therein we can glory; there's no end to it. We can glory in the cross of our Lord Jesus Christ, where the world is crucified unto us and we unto the world. We are a separated people, whether we like it or not. And I like it. Do you? I look at you, do you? Are you glad that the world is crucified unto you and you unto the world? We live a different life. The church lives a different life.

I hear preachers talking about the world out there, that the world is wicked. We know that. We know the world is on its way to the pit. I pray for those people out there. Pray for that sinner because he's lost, he's lost. And the Bible talks about hell fire! He's lost! We'd like to see those people turn to the Lord Jesus Christ. Let's do our part, let's pray! But while it's important to pray, you know what else is important then? That we walk upright. That we walk straight. So we go downtown, we go to

Walmart, and there we are. They see a difference in us, they see something about us people and they wonder, what is this all about? It's Jesus Christ that makes the difference. It's Jesus Christ, it's the Trinity that makes the difference in our life. Somebody left down years ago, that's why we have these nations that know not God. Think of those poor people. They don't know God. I'm not the judge. But what about the people that say they are church people, born-again people, and they cause someone to stumble? What about the preachers? Preachers are included, and maybe first of all. It's life, and life is serious. Life is no child's play. Because we have a head, and the head is the Lord Jesus Christ.

Now what made my hands go like this here? Because I turned my foot, then my hands went that way? No, no, it's because of the head. Let's get this really straight; the church functions according to the head, and the head is Jesus Christ. So we turn as the body. Some people might be the little toe. Oh, what's the little toe mean? I knew a man—he passed away years ago—he had his little toe cut off. You know what? He had to learn how to walk. That little toe helped him balance his life. So maybe I'm the little toe, I don't know. I don't know where we fit in. But if we are born again, we fit into the body of the Lord Jesus Christ. We fit in there! And there's where we want to function properly, and be a light to this world.

The Bible says we're the light of the world and the salt of the earth. What does salt do? It preserves food. Oh, and it makes desirable. It makes it tasty, doesn't it? Is that what we do when we go out and meet the people? Do they have a desire to live like we do?

We had an emphatic preacher this morning and I could have shouted a little bit, but we don't shout in church, right? We shout a little bit at home sometimes, you know. I read the word of God, I get a little excited, and when I'm by myself I do a little shouting and I do a little walking around and saying, "Praise God that for this old wretched sinner that used to use God's name in vain, He has taken the cursing and the anger out of me."

Don't you think I get an inspiration by reading the word of God? Get angry; why do you get angry? Oh, people get angry. You know, something happens in the home, in the car, and people get angry. Why do you get angry? The Bible says, "Be angry and sin not." The Bible says to put off anger, wrath and malice. You know, it tells us exactly how to live. The kingdom of God is within man. And with that kingdom—I'll repeat myself—that kingdom has a king. And that King is the Lord Jesus Christ. And He has the power, He has the authority to tell us which way to go. He's there to do that. Let's do it, by His grace.

There's work to be done for the church. Let's do it. The church is saying, "Come, come, accept the Lord Jesus Christ. Be converted." We don't have to tell people, "Oh, you shouldn't curse. You shouldn't smoke. You shouldn't go here, you shouldn't go there." Tell them about the love of God, and they'll be amazed and they'll say, "How does the Bible work? How you know the Bible is the Word of God? How do you know the Bible is true?" I'll tell you how. It works, it works. In that kingdom, you have the fruit of the spirit. The first fruit of the spirit is love. We have love for God. We have love for the Trinity; we have love for the church. We have love for our neighbor. He can steal your stones and take it across over to his land and make a flowerbed. You love the neighbor; you don't go out and say, "Oh, that fellow took my stones and made a flower bed on his side!" No, you love him. Why can you love him? Because you got the love of God! Love, then you got joy because you are witnessing, you're out there telling people of the Lord Jesus Christ. And you have love, joy, peace, longsuffering, gentleness, meekness... there's no end to that. There's absolutely no end to that. We can exercise that as long as we want to.

Then I want to come back yet to the parents. Husband, do you love your wife? Wife, you love your husband? Parents, you love your children? Children, do you love your parents?

Love, love in the home is beautiful. Love, joy, peace, longsuffering, gentleness, meekness, and temperance, all that; we're a balanced people enjoying ourselves in the Lord Jesus Christ. Friends, may the grace of our Lord Jesus Christ be upon your spirit.

THIS IS WHAT DAD MEANT WHEN HE SAID...

"...WE HAVE TO LIVE BY WHAT THIS WORD SAYS."

You hear or read the Word of God and somewhere deep inside it rings true; you know that you want—you need—the truth that you are hearing and seeing.

If, at that moment, you believe and acknowledge that Jesus is who He says He is and will do what He says He will do, He will forgive you and come to live in you by His Spirit.[1]

Christ took your sins on Himself, paid the price through His death on the cross, and rose again in victory over death. When you believe in Him, your sins are forgiven, your guilt and shame are erased, and you are freed from the power of sin in your life.[2]

You will be truly alive for the first time, and in a personal relationship with your Father and Creator. This does not mean everything will go perfectly; it means that you have a friend that will never leave you.[3]

His Spirit that lives in you will guide you in your life, comfort you in distress, and reveal God's heart to you.[4]

1. *That if thou shalt confess with thy mouth the Lord Jesus, and shalt believe in thine heart that God hath raised him from the dead, thou shalt be saved. For with the heart man believeth unto righteousness; and with the mouth confession is made unto salvation. (Romans 10:9, 10)*

2. *For sin shall not have dominion over you: for ye are not under the law, but under grace. (Romans 6:14)*

3. *...I will never leave thee, nor forsake thee. So that we may boldly say, The Lord is my Helper, and I will not fear what man shall do unto me. (Hebrews 13:5, 6)*

4. *Howbeit when he, the Spirit of truth is come, he will guide you into all truth: for he shall not speak of himself; but whatsoever he shall hear, that shall he speak: and he will show you things to come. (John 16:13)*

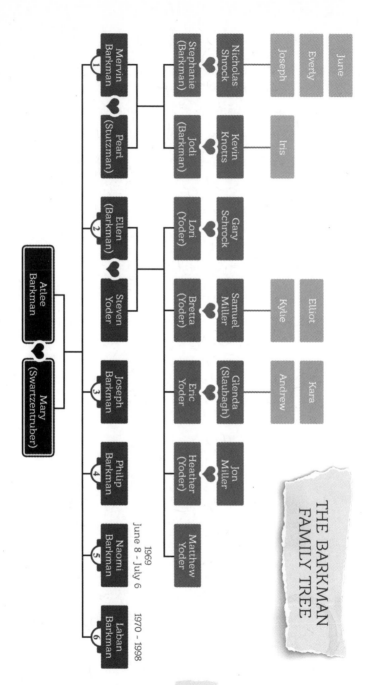

THE BARKMAN
FAMILY TREE

Atlee Barkman ♥ Mary (Swartzentruber)

1 Mervin Barkman ♥ Pearl (Stutzman)
- Stephanie (Barkman) ♥ Nicholas Shrock
  - Joseph
  - Everly
  - June
- Jodi (Barkman) ♥ Kevin Knotts
  - Iris

2 Ellen (Barkman) ♥ Steven Yoder
- Lori (Yoder) ♥ Gary Schrock
- Bretta (Yoder) ♥ Samuel Miller
  - Kyle
  - Elliot
- Eric Yoder ♥ Glenda (Slaubagh)
  - Andrew
  - Kara
- Heather (Yoder) ♥ Jon Miller
- Matthew Yoder

3 Joseph Barkman

4 Philip Barkman

5 Naomi Barkman
1969 June 8 - July 6

6 Laban Barkman
1970 - 1998

206

Last family photo, 2016
Merv, Ellen, Joe, Phil, Atlee, Mary

Atlee and Mary with their great-grandchildren, 2016

Merv and Pearl

Merv and Pearl's Family

Steve and Ellen

Steve and Ellen's Family

Phil and Joe